People everywhere are discovering the magic of MINDMAPPING!

"IF YOU'RE TIRED OF JUST MINDYAPPING, OR WORSE, MINDNAPPING, YOU OWE IT TO YOURSELF TO READ AND PRACTICE THE TECHNIQUES OF MINDMAPPING."

—Eugene Raudsepp, President,
Princeton Creative Research, Inc.

"MINDMAPPING . . . HAS CHANGED MY LIFE, ALLOWING ME THE ABILITY TO CAPTURE MY CREATIVE FLOW, THEN ORGANIZE IT AND BE ABLE TO PUT THOSE CREATIVE JUICES TO GOOD USE. THIS BOOK IS *MUST* READING FOR ANYONE WHO HAS AN INTEREST IN BEING MORE CREATIVE, INNOVATIVE AND PRODUCTIVE."

—G. Lynne Snead, Director,
Franklin International Institute

"A POWERFUL TOOL TO HELP ACHIEVE PEAK PERFORMANCE . . . IN ALL ASPECTS OF OUR LIVES."

—Charles Garfield, author and speaker,
Peak Performance & Peak Performers

Continued . . .

"OF GREAT VALUE TO ANYONE WHO MUST REMAIN FUNCTIONAL IN TODAY'S WORLD. THIS BOOK . . . SHOWS THE MANY USES AND EXAMPLES OF HOW TO USE MINDMAPPING IN EVERYDAY LIFE."

—Tom McDaniel, Vice President,
Amtech Systems Corporation

"A SIMPLE, STRAIGHTFORWARD WAY TO CAPTURE IDEAS, CREATE PATHS FOR THEIR EVOLUTION, AND DEVELOP METHODS TO IMPLEMENT THEM. YOU CAN ONLY ACHIEVE WHAT YOU CAN IMAGINE—THIS BOOK WILL HELP."

—Jon Nakatani, Human Resources Consultant

"HOW COULD ANYONE RESIST KNOWING HOW TO BE MORE CREATIVE? . . . THIS BOOK PRESENTS MINDMAPPING IN A CLEAR AND UNDERSTANDABLE FORMAT."

—Bobbi DePorter, President,
Learning Forum/SuperCamp

"MY ONLY WISH IS THAT I HAD DISCOVERED MINDMAPPING YEARS AGO. NOT ONLY DO I HIGHLY RECOMMEND IT TO ANY FRIENDS, BUT I'VE ALSO TAUGHT OUR FOUR CHILDREN. THANKS!"

—Stew Leonard, Stew Leonard's Dairy Store

"WELL WRITTEN, LIBERALLY SPRINKLED WITH TOOLS, TECHNIQUES AND IDEAS."

—Arlan Tietel, Training Manager, *3M*

"IF YOU WANT TO ENHANCE YOUR RELATIONSHIP WITH YOUR ASSOCIATES, YOUR FAMILY, BUT MOST IMPORTANTLY, YOURSELF, READ WYCOFF'S BOOK ON MINDMAPPING TODAY!"

—Barney Sofro, Chairman, House of Fabrics

MINDMAPPING®

Your Personal Guide to Exploring Creativity and Problem-Solving

JOYCE WYCOFF

BERKLEY BOOKS, NEW YORK

Grateful acknowledgment is given to the following for permission for quoted material:

From *The Three Pound Universe* by Judith Hooper and Dick Teresi. Copyright © 1986 by Dick Teresi and Judith Hooper. Reprinted with permission of Macmillan Publishing Company.

From *Moments of Truth* by Jan Carlzon. Copyright © 1987 by Ballinger Publishing Company. Used by permission of Harper Business, a division of HarperCollins Publishers.

From *Kids Who Succeed* by Beverly Neuer Feldman. Copyright © 1987 by Beverly Neuer Feldman. Reprinted with permission of Writers House Inc.

From *Thinking Visually: A Strategy Manual for Problem Solving* by Robert H. McKim. Copyright © 1980 by Robert H. McKim. Used with permission of Van Nostrand Reinhold.

Mindmapping® is a registered trademark belonging to Tony Buzan.

MINDMAPPING®

A Berkley Book / published by arrangement with the author

PRINTING HISTORY
Berkley trade paperback edition / June 1991

For information address: The Berkley Publishing Group, 200 Madison Avenue, New York, New York 10016.

ISBN: 0-425-12780-X

BERKLEY®
Berkley Books are published by The Berkley Publishing Group, 200 Madison Avenue, New York, New York 10016.
BERKLEY and the "B" design are trademarks belonging to Berkley Publishing Corporation.

PRINTED IN THE UNITED STATES OF AMERICA

20 19 18 17 16 15 14

Dedicated to:

Tamara, who lit the spark and tends the flame;

Richard, who brightens all my hours and provides unlimited support and encouragement;

Stephanie and Annie, who bring me joy and new vistas,

And, **Mom and Dad,** who told me I could when I was too young to know better.

I love you all!!

Acknowledgments

I used to wonder why books always started off with the author thanking so many people. Now I know. This book reflects the work, love and support of many people. Thank you to all of you who read, revised, corrected and improved the manuscript.

Thanks to Lynne Snead, who provided immense support and friendship; to Jeff Herman, my favorite literary agent; to Anne Durrum Robinson who led me to Jeff, and who is a guiding inspiration; to Brad Winch, who gave me the confidence to tackle the project; to Steve Cook, the artist who polished the mindmaps for the book; to Trish Todd and Jennifer Enderlin, for their excellent editing and support; and to all the workshop participants who fell in love with mindmapping and convinced me of its power and importance.

Thanks also to the geniuses who invented personal computers, WordPerfect and Ventura Publishing.

But perhaps most of all, thanks to the giants who have cleared the path for me. To all the scientists who have begun to unravel the mysteries of our remarkable brain and all the writers and researchers who have developed techniques and methods that allow us to further develop and explore our potential. Special thanks to Roger Sperry, Karl Pribram, Edward de Bono, Tony Buzan, Peter Russell, Alex Osborn, Ned Hermann, Betty Edwards, Marilyn Ferguson, Charles Garfield, Willis Harmon and . . . and the list is endless but thanks to all of you who have added to the growing body of knowledge about our brain and its vast potential.

Contents

Chapter 3: Mindmapping: Whole Brain Thinking Technique (continued)

Foreword

How great is your brain power and how much of it do you use?

In the 1950s, psychologists estimated that the average person used 50 percent of brain capacity. In the '60s and '70s, the estimate was lowered to 10 percent. In the '80s, it declined to one percent. Now, in the 1990s, the best guess is .01 percent or less.

These estimates are not a reflection of deteriorating global intelligence but rather an expression of our increasingly sophisticated ability to measure the brain's vast potential. One of the world's most prominent brain researchers, Professor Pyotor Anokhin, published a scientific estimate of the number of possible thought patterns of which the average human brain is capable. The estimate, which he stressed was conservative, was considerably greater than the number of atoms in the entire universe.

In the pages that follow, Joyce Wycoff guides you through an exciting exploration of the power of the brain. Of course, an understanding of our potential can provide inspiration and motivation, but inspiration and motivation alone are insufficient; we need a practical guide for gaining access to our untapped abilities. *Mindmapping* offers a practical and immediately applicable introduction to mindmapping—a remarkably powerful system for harnessing our brain power.

Mindmapping was developed in the early 1970s by Tony Buzan as a tool to help people take notes more effectively. As he applied the tool, he realized that he had discovered not just a better way of note taking, but a new and powerful means of improving his students' thinking skills.

The value of mindmapping is perhaps best understood in contrast with the technique most of us learned for generating our ideas and taking notes: the traditional outline. However, outlining demands that we order ideas before giving free reign to the process of idea generation, thereby interfering with the speed and range of our idea production.

Our brains possess unlimited potential for idea generation. They work best when we allow our ideas to flow freely before attempting to organize. While numerous non linear note taking systems have evolved to free the mind to generate ideas before having to organize them, mindmapping goes beyond these systems. Mindmapping provides a systematic means for recording and encouraging the natural flow of the thinking process by creating a "positive feedback loop" between brain and notes.

Try this: Think about the last book you read and imagine that you have to write a report on it. As you begin to recall ideas, you will probably not see a formal outline in your mind's eye. Rather, you get key words, associations, pictures and images that seem to "float up to consciousness." In order to produce your report, you will ultimately have to organize these streams of association.

In addition to enhancing the freedom of association, mindmapping provides an innovative, comprehensive approach to idea organization. Many of our students comment that mindmapping seems natural, that they've devised their own note taking system involving images, colors and key words that approximate mindmapping. They are thrilled to discover that their own intuitions have been developed and systemized in a way that allows them to explore new dimensions of flexibility and precision of thought.

Since 1975, I have worked closely with Buzan, developing mindmapping as a tool for training people to think more powerfully. In the late 1970s we created a vision: that 100 million people would be using mindmapping regularly by the year 2000, that mindmapping would be taught in schools and become part of the regular working process of corporate life. To realize this vision requires individuals to teach, express and communicate the power of mindmapping in different ways.

Joyce Wycoff's book is a valuable contribution to this realization. With sincerity and thoughtfulness, she has created a commonsense introductory manual for mindmapping, demonstrating its practical application to a wide variety of life skills.

Mindmapping has recently become a "hot topic" and many people are jumping on its bandwagon. But all too often their treatment of the subject is superficial and exploitative. The power of mindmapping is often misunderstood because the technique is so simple that one can easily miss its deeper meanings. Joyce Wycoff's flexibility and willingness to think through the issues about which she writes sets this book apart from most other efforts on the subject.

One of the beauties of Joyce's work is that she has applied the thinking skills about which she is writing to the actual writing of the book. As you read the pages that follow and apply what you learn, you will gain ever increasing access to your own magnificent mind!

Michael J. Gelb,
Founder and President,
High Performance Learning
Washington, D.C.,
Summer 1990

Introduction: Mouse Diapers and Rainbows

"Mouse diapers"
". . . little, tiny mouse diapers."
"packaged twelve to a box . . ."
"prefolded and powdered . . ."
". . . with optional home delivery."
"They'll be the biggest thing since pet rocks."
"We'll be rich!"

Giggles and guffaws mingled with the voices of several people calling out ideas and comments all at once.

Who are these people and why are they talking about mouse diapers? A teenage slumber party? A Pictionary game?

No, this group is actually a new product development team at a division of Hewlett-Packard . . . in the middle of a mindmapping session.

Are mouse diapers HP's new secret product?

No, but mindmapping is helping them develop their new products.

So what is this mindmapping? And what's it got to do with new product development?

I'm glad you asked.

The rainbows of the mind brighten the skies of our life with color, grace and contrast against stormy clouds.

Where do the *rainbows of the mind* come from?—those brilliant flashes of color and grace and beauty that light up our life? The brain has been analyzed and mapped, dissected and probed, stained and photographed. Knowledge about its multitude of electrical connections and chemical reactions is increasing astronomically. And yet, these unique interactions which comprise our mind remain a mystery. While we have a better understanding of the process that leads to rainbows . . . to creativity . . . , the brain is so complex that we may never understand its operations completely.

The brain is nature's marvelous gift—our entire universe is created in this three pounds of wrinkled matter—everything we see and hear, everything we taste and touch, every emotion we feel, every movement we make, every thought and inspiration happens because of our brain.

New challenges need new solutions

The world around us is changing rapidly—so rapidly that we almost feel that we are constantly in a strange, new land. This new land demands new solutions and approaches to its challenges. Our primary tool in this new land is our mind . . . our imagination and creativity.

It is our imagination and creativity which will open the doors to progress, to new products and services, to new worldwide markets, to new ways of communicating, to new ways of preserving our environment and resources. It is our imagination and creativity which will bring us more beauty, more music, better schools, more jobs, homes for the homeless and an end to hunger and war. In the search for understanding our mind, we need tools that have not been part of our standard education and experience, tools that will open up the territory of our mind.

Mindmapping: the magical tool

Mindmapping is one of those tools. It is a technique for developing a more creative and innovative approach to thinking. Mindmapping has an almost magical effect; it taps into the whole brain, allows projects to be organized in minutes, promotes creativity, breaks writer's block and provides an effective mechanism for doing brainstorming.

Mindmapping is easy to learn and use. By the end of Chapter 3, you will know enough about mindmapping to immediately improve your writing abilities, enhance your project organization skills and utilize your time more effectively. The rest of the book will show you additional ways to use mindmapping.

Self-discovery workbook

This is a workbook—not a textbook. Each application of the mindmapping technique is followed by several exercises. The exercises take only a few minutes. Try them, play with them. They will reveal parts of you that you may never have seen before. That's what this is all about: discovering new things about yourself through mindmapping. Until we discover who we truly are, we will not be able to unfold our full potential and creativity.

You are invited to use this book and the mindmapping technique on your journey of discovery. It will give you a better appreciation of the power of your mind. As you begin to use this magical technique, your perspective will broaden and you will become a better thinker.

This book is organized into three sections:

Section One—Understanding the Brain and Creativity

Mindmapping is based on brain/mind research and principles. This section explains the operations of the brain, how creativity works and how mindmapping organizes these principles into a powerful information processing, idea generating technique.

Section Two—Techniques of Mindmapping

Mindmapping is a simple technique, yet each element of the technique is important. This section explains each element from the basics to advanced mindmapping.

Section Three—Applications of Mindmapping

Mindmapping is an extremely versatile, powerful technique. This section shows you the most common applications of mindmapping and may trigger new ways for you to use it.

Welcome to mindmapping and a different way of looking at the world around us! Who knows, you may find that discovering mouse diapers can be fun!

SECTION ONE

Understanding the Brain and Creativity

Chapter 1: The Mind's Unknown Potential

Capacities clamor to be used and cease their clamor only when they are well used.
—A. H. Maslow

The brain . . . the last frontier

As the Enterprise speeds away into the darkness, a somber voice begins the introduction with . . . "Space . . . the final frontier."

There is another vast, uncharted frontier—one much closer to home . . . our own mind. The dimensions of this frontier are almost as overwhelming as space. Within the three pounds of gray, wrinkled brain mass are between 10 and 15 BILLION nerve cells capable of making 10^{800} connections! Most of us have no way of comprehending what that potential means—it is inconceivably large. Richard Restak, M.D., in his book *The Brain*, states "the human brain can store more information than all the libraries in the world."

The brain creates our universe

In *The Three-Pound Universe*, Judith Hooper and Dick Teresi compare the brain to the universe. They state, "In fact, it *is* the known universe. Everything we know—from subatomic particles to distant galaxies—everything we feel—from love for our children to fear of enemy nations—is experienced and modeled in our brains. Without the brain, nothing—not quarks, not black holes, nor love, nor hatred—would exist for us."

Many of our great thinkers, including Aristotle, believed that the mind was located in the stomach or heart area. Plato placed the mind in the brain . . . but only because of the brain's shape. Most of our information about the brain has been discovered in the past 20 years, but this knowledge has only begun to open our awareness to the awesome complexity of the brain.

We frequently compare our brain to a computer: it has input, it has processing through a central processor, and it has output. Computers are the model of bit by bit, logical processing. As computers became more and more powerful, the brain seemed almost a pale version of their lightning speed and power. A comparison of the brain and a computer could look like Figure 1.

Pattern Recognition

However, as knowledge of both the brain and computers increased, scientists realized that a computer was not just a bigger and better brain. There were things the brain could do that computers couldn't seem to do at all. For example, if we go to our high school reunion after 20 years and run into Harry, who is bald and 30 pounds heavi-

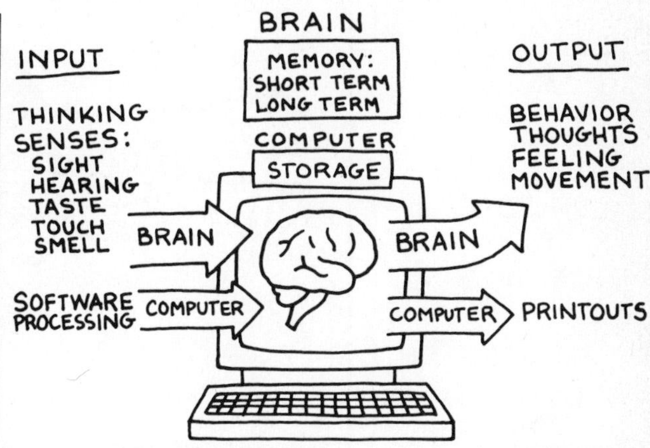

Figure 1: Computer/Brain Comparison

er than the last time we saw him, the chances are good that we will still recognize him. A computer wouldn't. Our recognition of Harry is based on *pattern recognition.* If we hear the first three or four notes of the "Wedding March," we instantly recognize the song. This is *pattern completion.* We do it easily; computers do it with great difficulty, if at all. If we see a word mizspld, we still understand what it says. This is *pattern correction,* and again, it is almost impossible for a computer.

The difference: pattern recognition

Robert Heinlein in *Stranger in a Strange Land* uses the term "grok." To grok means to understand completely all at once. When something is "grokked," its pattern is understood completely as a gestalt. To date, computers cannot "grok."

Computers can't "grok"

The brain can also handle ambiguity. What do you see in this drawing from Robert H. McKim's *Thinking Visually*? Most people eventually see two patterns—a duck and a rabbit. The mind receives enough information to complete two pat-

Ambiguity stimulates more brain connections

Example of Ambiguity in Pattern Recognition

terns and can switch back and forth between the two interpretations of the picture until it decides which pattern it wants to use.

Mind as a Jelly Dish

Edward de Bono, author of many books on the mind and the thinking process, uses an analogy which perfectly describes how the pattern recognition process works and how a creative idea is born.

De Bono compares the mind to a dish of jelly which has settled so that its surface is perfectly flat. When information enters the mind, it self-organizes. It is like pouring warm water on the dish of jelly with a teaspoon. Imagine the warm water being poured on the jelly dish and then gently tipped so that it runs off. After many repetitions of this process, the surface of the jelly would be full of ruts, indentations and grooves.

New water (information) would start to automatically flow into the preformed grooves. After a while, it would take only a little bit of information (water) to activate an entire channel. This is the pattern recognition and pattern completion process. When information enters the mind it falls into a channel, a pattern. Even if much of the information is outside the channel, the pattern will be activated. The mind automatically "corrects" and "completes" the information to select and activate a pattern.

Information self-organizes in the brain

Creativity occurs when we tilt the jelly dish and force some of the water (information) to flow into new channels and make new connections. This process of creativity will be discussed further in the next chapter.

Creativity comes when information makes new connections

One Brain or Two?

In the early 1960s, Roger Sperry, an experimental psychologist at California Institute of Technology, performed landmark experiments with people suffering from epilepsy. Assuming that their seizures were the result of erratic electrical impulses between brain hemispheres, he severed the corpus callosum which connects the brain hemispheres. In a sense, the operations were a success as the seizures were eliminated and the patients were well and functioning.

However, Sperry's studies revealed some unusual aftereffects of the operation and demonstrated the importance of hemispheric communication and the existence of hemispheric specialization. Sperry and his associate, Michael S. Gazzaniga, who later won the Nobel Prize for their split-brain studies, discovered that when they flashed a picture of an

Sperry disconnected the two halves of the brain

apple in such a way that it was seen only by the right visual field (thus, the left brain hemisphere), the patient could immediately identify and name the apple. The same slide shown to the left visual field and projected to the right hemisphere could not be named. The studies gradually revealed that the right hemisphere did not possess the language skills necessary to identify the symbol (word) for apple. However, when asked to retrieve the object shown, the patient's left hand (controlled by the right hemisphere) could pick out the apple. The right brain was recognizing the object but was unable to produce the word identifying it.

Gradually, the specializations of each hemisphere were identified as having these traits:

Each brain hemisphere has a set of specific traits

Left Brain—Language, logic, numbers, sequence, looks at details, linear, symbolic representation, judgmental

Right Brain—Images, rhythm, music, imagination, color, looks at the whole, patterns, emotions, nonjudgmental

The split-brain studies revealed a part of the brain that had been hidden, a part that recognized patterns, that responded to music, rhythm and emotions, a part that was primarily visual and imaginative. These qualities of the brain became known as "right brain" traits.

"Right brain" and "left brain" are shorthand terms for the traits represented

In the past few years, the term "right brain" has become a faddish way of saying creative, artistic and "neat" as opposed to the supposedly dull, analytical, stolid opposite, "left brain." Unfortunately, the term has added to current psychobabble and has been shrouded with a veil of misinformation. Although it is true that the brain has two hemispheres, each with its own spe-

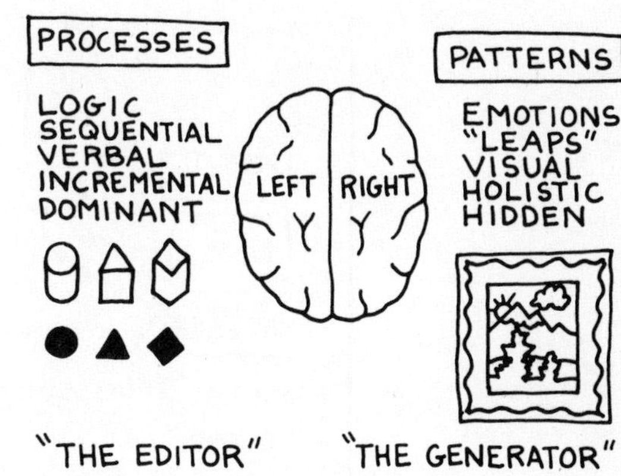

Traits of the Hemispheres

cializations, being "right brained" is neither better nor worse than being "left brained." The important thing to remember is that "right brain" and "left brain" are simply shorthand, or a metaphor, for the specialities which tend to be handled by the respective sides of the brain. Both sets of traits are critical to our thinking processes. Creativity results from the exceptional interaction between both hemispheres rather than being a product of the right hemisphere.

Creativity comes from exceptional interaction of both "brains"

Right brain traits are emphasized in order to counterbalance our education system, which has tended to stress the left brain traits of memory, language skills, arithmetic, logical thought and sequence. We have been taught to find and regurgitate the "right" answer, and until recently, schools provided little opportunity to exercise imagination and alternative thinking skills. Therefore, in trying to develop a more "whole brained" approach, we often emphasize the right brain skills—not because they are more important

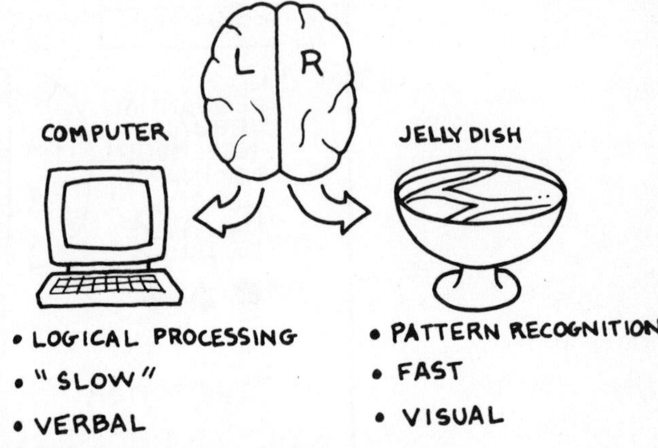

Figure 2: Computer/Whole Brain Comparison

but because we have had less opportunity to use them.

With the addition of the pattern recognition skills, the computer/brain comparison can be updated to look like Figure 2.

Memory . . . How Much? Where?

Peter Russell in *The Brain Book* states that Xerxes could recall the 100,000 men in his army by name, that Cardinal Mezzofanti knew 70 to 80 languages and that Polish Jews known as Shass Pollaks routinely knew every word and every page of the twelve large volumes of the Talmud. So why don't I remember the name of the person just introduced to me?

Memory consists of storage and recall

There are actually two parts of the memory process—storage and recall. Many researchers now believe that we store everything that we experience in our lives. Although this seems physically impossible, the hologram theory of memory makes this belief seem a little more feasible.

Memory as a hologram

The dominant theory of memory uses a hologram analogy and was developed by Karl Pribram of Stanford Medical School. When you embark on a trip through Disneyland's Haunted House, one of the most memorable sights you see is that of a ghostly young girl, miniaturized and trapped in a plastic cage. She is forever young, forever trapped, forever calling for someone to help her. 3-D images such as these are created by splitting a laser beam with part of the beam going directly to a photographic plate and part going to an image where it is then reflected onto the plate.

Image is stored throughout the plate

While these pictures are amazing, the truly incredible aspect of holograms is that the image is included in each part of the photographic plate. If the plate is broken, the whole image can be reproduced from any piece of the plate. The image is actually distributed throughout the plate through the storage of waves.

Memory could not be found in any one brain location

Pribram worked briefly in the 1950s with Karl Lashley, who was searching for the engram, the exact location of a memory. The search for engrams was unsuccessful, but the hologram suggested a possible storage mechanism to Pribram. He suggests that memories are not stored in specific neurons but are distributed throughout the whole brain somewhat in the same manner as a hologram. Karl Lashley's experiments support this theory of memory. He trained rats to run mazes and then removed parts of their brain. Regardless of which part was removed, the memory remained.

Physicist David Bohm uses the hologram as an analogy for the entire universe, stating that reality is pure vibration and every part a representation of the whole. William Blake once talked of "seeing the whole world in a grain of sand." Perhaps he had the same vision as Bohm.

Unlimited storage capacity

If we believe that memories are stored in the same manner as holograms, we have a mechanism for understanding the brain's capacity. According to Peter Russell, one cubic centimeter of a photographic hologram can store ten billion bits of information—the human brain is 1,500 times as large. He estimates that the human memory capacity is on the order of a quadrillion (1,000 million-million!?) bits of information. Of course a great deal of this is taken up by the programs necessary to run our bodies, but it still leaves plenty of capacity for remembering all our experiences.

Some fascinating studies have been done to test this theory. Direct stimulation of the brain has elicited whole memories rich in detail. One report comes from Yale, where a bricklayer was tested under hypnosis and was able to describe a specific brick he had laid for a building. Even though he had laid 2,000 bricks a day, he was able to describe the brick's color and flaws in detail. The experimenter was later able to verify those details.

Hypnosis reveals enormous memory storage . . . including memories of birth

David B. Chamberlain, Ph.D., a psychologist in San Diego, studied birth memories and found remarkable, detailed memories. He separately interviewed mothers and their children, under hypnosis, to obtain detailed descriptions of the birth moment. The high level of correlation between the stories and verified details present in the child's memories, indicate the presence of a full set of memories from the moment of birth.

Recall: the key to memory

If we are storing everything that happens to us, what causes us to be unable to recall all of this detail? The primary cause of forgetting seems to be interference. As experiences are piled on top of each other, the memories interfere with each other and the search process breaks down for lack of clear-cut associations and patterns. The retrieval keys are lost.

There are four primary tools for improving memory recall and learning:

Repetition—The standard tool of our education system. Rote learning works but may not be the most effective method and is definitely not the only method.

Association/Connection—Linking a piece of information with something already established in our memory allows us to recall the information and use it in other contexts.

Intensity—Information which has intensity or emotional content will be more readily recalled than other information. If your health and well-being depended on your remembering "Sam Spade stood staring, still Sally stole stilts," you would probably remember it quite easily.

Involvement—Information which involves more than one of our senses will be remembered more easily than information experienced by just one of our senses. If you can see something, hear it, touch it, taste it and smell it, you will more likely remember it than if you just saw it. Working with information, writing it down, organizing it or adding associations to it all help you remember and understand the material.

To remember names: repeat and link

Perhaps this explains why I can't remember the name of the person just introduced to me—I heard the name only once. If I was busy trying to figure out what I was going to say next, I may not have heard the name at all. To increase my chances of remembering that name, I should repeat the name and associate the name with an image. This takes a little time at first, but the time itself is a form of involvement. As you develop a library of name images, it takes less time.

One of the best methods of increasing your recall abilities when learning new material (books, meetings, lectures, etc.) is mindmapping. Note taking with mindmapping requires an involvement with the material which naturally creates strong memory patterns. It creates images, allows you to organize the material as it is received, makes associations and connects with material from other sources.

Mindmapping actively engages both hemispheres of our brains. By allowing us to freely interact with information, and by adding color, symbols and organization to the information as we receive it, mindmapping helps us develop the full potential of our minds. We develop better memories, more powerful organizational skills and more creativity.

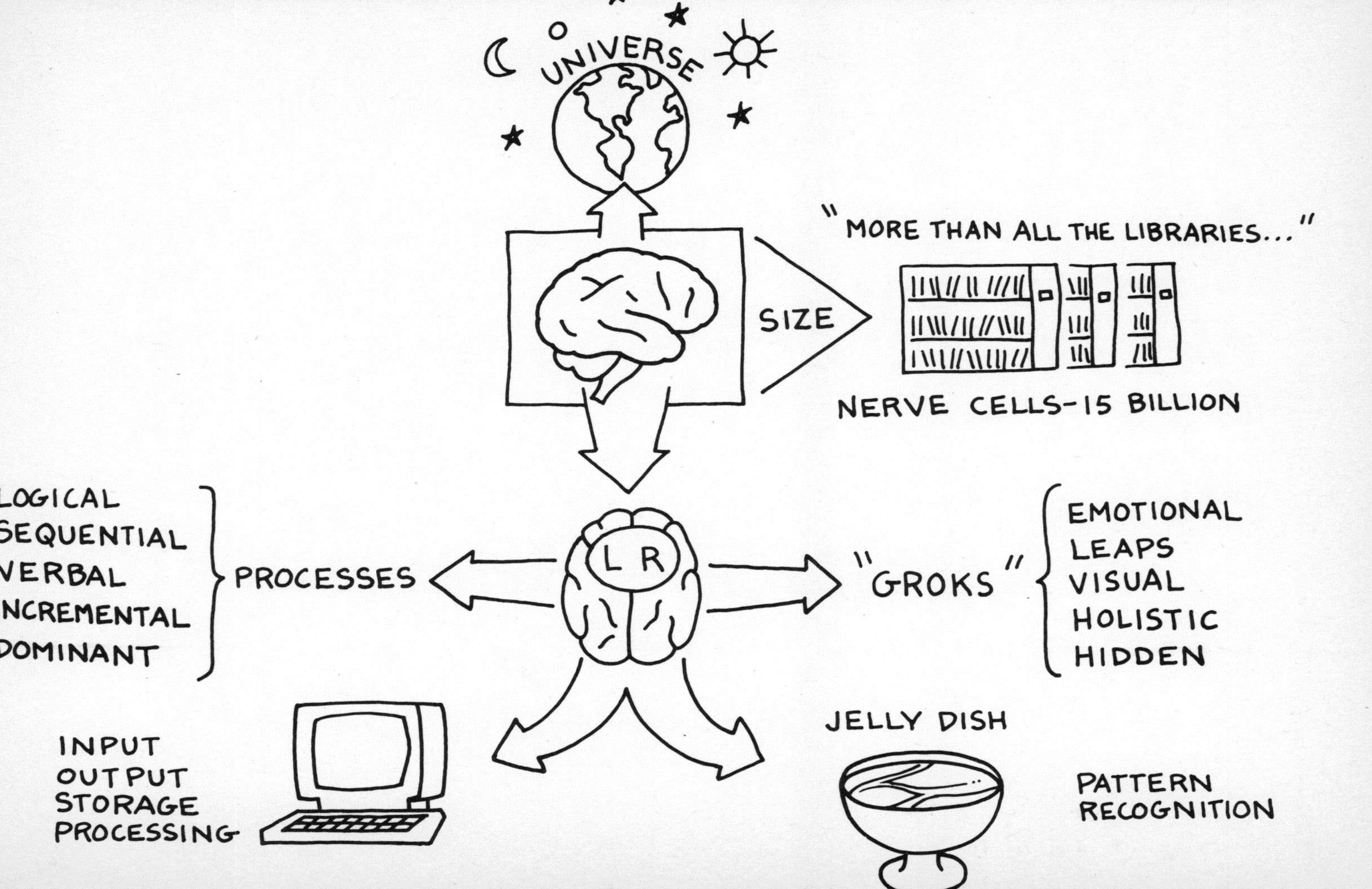

UNIVERSE
SIZE
"MORE THAN ALL THE LIBRARIES..."
NERVE CELLS-15 BILLION
L R
LOGICAL
SEQUENTIAL
VERBAL
INCREMENTAL
DOMINANT
PROCESSES
"GROKS"
EMOTIONAL
LEAPS
VISUAL
HOLISTIC
HIDDEN
INPUT
OUTPUT
STORAGE
PROCESSING
JELLY DISH
PATTERN
RECOGNITION

Chapter 2: Creativity—Within Each of Us

Creativity is piercing the mundane to find the marvelous.
—Bill Moyers

Creativity is seeing things that everyone around us sees while making connections that no one else has made.

Each of us is inherently creative

Often when we discuss creativity, we refer only to the works of the great artists . . . the paintings of van Gogh, the music of Mozart, the sonnets of Shakespeare. But while these masters displayed extraordinary talent and creativity, it does not mean that the rest of us are lacking in creativity. However, as we go through life, we tend to lose our ability to get in touch with our creative nature.

Beverly Neuer Feldman, author of *Kids Who Succeed*, tells of her early art training:

> When I was in elementary school, my art class homework consisted of pasting a tiny reprint of

an old-master painting on a piece of construction paper. The teacher's directions were most explicit about how many inches to leave for margins. We never discussed the paintings in class, but we certainly discussed those margins. We were graded on how accurately we had measured them. (This particular art activity is still going on in classrooms today.) By the time I reached high school I hated art. Take an art course? Never! And so I joined the ranks of the many others who say, "I'm not creative"—a self-condemnation that decreased my measure of self-worth.

What I did not understand then was that the only real distinction between the creative and uncreative is the fact that the former have grown up to consider themselves creative and the latter have not.

Creativity—What Is It?

Creativity: new and useful solutions

How, then, do we define this quality that lies within us? Standard answers usually include: "new"; "a different way of doing something"; "unique"; "different"; "better." Our preferred definition is simply: "New and useful." To be creative implies bringing new meaning or purpose to a task, finding new uses, solving existing problems or adding beauty or value. Therefore, it is as possible to be a creative homemaker as it is to be a creative writer. Creativity is as useful to a parent in dealing with a child as it is to an artist painting a picture or a business person creating a new product.

Due to the phenomenal complexity of our genetic makeup and the uniqueness of each life experience, we are as distinct as snowflakes. This dissimilarity is the basis for our creativity. We each have a unique perspective to express, a completely different set of talents and experiences to translate through our individual skills. It is the process of finding and listening to that individual perspective which results in the expression of our creativity. Creativity is actually translating our voice or our "self" into tangible expressions . . . works of art, music, solutions to problems in our careers, children, flair in decorating our homes, style in dress, hobbies, dance or other expressive activities.

Creativity is the expression of our uniqueness

The difficult part of creativity is recognizing our own unique voice and respecting it. As we evolved into "civilized" animals living in groups, distinctness became a liability. The individual acting alone was at more risk and could become a hazard for the community. Individualism was discouraged. Group conformity was easier and safer. "Groupthink" was invented.

Man's duality: the desire to be part of a group and maintain individuality

As strong as group pressure is, however, we do not easily give up our individuality. The urge to creativity is seen all around us . . . in our homes and wardrobes . . . in our hobbies, from knitting to baseball card collecting . . . in the bumper stickers we put on our cars. Everywhere we see the duality of man . . . the desire to be at once part of the group and, at the same time, a separate individual. Abraham Maslow called the urge to maximize our individual talents the desire for self-actualization. He said that each of us desires "to become everything that one is capable of becoming. *What man can be, he must be.*" (Author's italics.)

We must listen closely to discover our inner truth

One purpose of life is to discover who we are. Finding out who we are, though, is not as easy as it would seem. We are so much a part of the group that we have to listen very closely to discover our inner self . . . what our uniqueness is. It is when we finally hear the truth of ourselves that we discover our own creativity. This process of self-discovery is as important as the possible products of that discovery. Mindmapping is an excellent technique to help you on this journey of self-discovery.

Your Untapped Creativity

Peter Dean, artist, is quoted in *Who's Who* as saying, "I'm a magician through whom the images of our time pass and become paintings. I'm an interpreter of reality into fantasy and back again. I'm a juggler of textures and color. I'm a seer of the past and a prophet of the future. ***I ride the hurricane, I walk the tightrope of sanity. I live on the edge of the world."*** (Author's emphasis.)

Creativity is the translation of our uniqueness into outward action

"I live on the edge of the world." That statement perfectly describes the feelings of the person who is delving into his or her inner soul . . . the person who is discovering the inner self and translating that inner uniqueness into outward actions.

A person who is striving to fulfill his potential, to use all of his capabilities, is described by Maslow as a self-actualized person. In his research, he found that the self-actualized person has several characteristic traits:

- Perceives reality accurately and objectively; tolerates and even likes ambiguity; and is not threatened by the unknown
- Accepts himself, others and human nature
- Is spontaneous, natural, genuine

Maslow's traits of the self-actualized person

- Is problem-centered (not self-centered), non-egotistical; has a philosophy of life and probably a mission in life
- Needs some privacy and solitude more than others do; is able to concentrate intensely
- Is independent, self-sufficient and autonomous; has less need for praise or popularity
- Has the capacity to appreciate simple and commonplace experiences; has zest in living, high humor, and the ability to handle stress
- Has (and is aware of) rich, alive, fulfilling "peak experiences"—moments of intense enjoyment
- Has deep feelings of brotherhood with all mankind; is benevolent, altruistic
- Forms strong friendship ties with relatively few people; and is capable of greater love
- Is democratic and unprejudiced in the deepest possible sense
- Is strongly ethical and moral in individual (not necessarily conventional) ways; enjoys work in achieving a goal as much as the goal itself; is patient, for the most part
- Has a thoughtful, philosophical sense of humor that is constructive, not destructive
- Is creative, original, inventive with a fresh, naive, simple and direct way of looking at life; tends to do most things creatively—but does not necessarily possess great talent
- Is capable of detachment from culture; can objectively compare cultures and can take or leave conventions

If we desire to strive for self-actualization, we can use these 15 traits as a blueprint for self-development. As much as anything else, the self-actualizing person has an overwhelming drive to discover his own possibilities . . . to push past his boundaries.

Jan Carlzon, CEO of Scandinavian Airline Systems, in *Moments of Truth*, talks about barriers: "I have a saying that helps shake off psychological barriers like these: *'Run through walls.'* (Author's italics). Your goal may seem impossible but don't stop trying to accomplish it until someone really says 'No.' The walls towering before you may not be as massive as they appear. Maybe they're not stone walls at all but cardboard facades that you can run straight through."

Question all barriers . . . they may be cardboard

Traits of Creative People

Many other scientists have studied creative people to discover common traits and to try to discover just what makes creativity. Most studies show the following four traits as common to creative people:

Courage—Creative people dare new tasks and are willing to risk failure. They are curious to see what will happen. Richard L. Weaver II, professor at Bowling Green University, once said, *"Creativity means willingness to frolic in new territory."*

Expressive—Creative people are not afraid to express their thoughts and feelings. They are willing to be themselves. T. J. Twitchell, a financial consultant with Merrill-Lynch, overcame her fear of "cold-calling" by standing up and wearing a baseball-style aviator's cap. It made her think of cold-calling as an adventure and helped her become one of Merrill-Lynch's top rookie brokers.

Humor—Humor is closely related to creativity. When we combine elements in a way that is different, unexpected and incongruous, we wind up with humor. Combining elements in ways that are new and useful produces creativity.

Intuition—Creative people accept their intuition as a legitimate aspect of their personality. They understand that much intuition comes from the right brain traits which do not have the same communication patterns as the left brain.

Other psychological traits identified by David N. Perkins, codirector of Harvard University's Project Zero, as being common to creative people are:

- A drive to find order in a chaotic situation
- An interest in finding unusual problems as well as solutions
- Ability to make new connections and challenge traditional assumptions
- The ability to balance idea creation with testing and judgment
- The desire to push the boundaries of their competence
- Motivation by the problem or task itself rather than external rewards such as money, grades or recognition

Creativity does not come from having "one right answer"

These traits can be taught and encouraged but our current educational system is so overwhelmed with limited budgets and with socioeconomic problems such as drugs, dropouts and teacher burnout, that not enough attention can be given to teaching students to think and be more creative. Students are not stimulated to find and define their own problems. Chaos is discouraged. Students are not taught to look for and value more than one answer to problems. There is too much emphasis on right answers and "safe" thinking.

Children are naturally creative, unconventional, humorous, and are easily bored. Our education system encourages discipline, conformity, silence and regurgitation of the answer the teacher wants to hear, so these traits are often stifled.

The school system that wants order and discipline and the child who complies with the system in order to avoid failure and ridicule jointly establish an environment of mediocrity. The fear of failure begins to dominate the child's natural curiosity. Creativity training erases the negative messages of our education system and allows people to get in touch with their originality.

Once people discover their creativity, they tend to be independent, self-confident, risk-taking, highly energetic, enthusiastic, spontaneous, adventurous, thorough, curious, humorous, playful, childlike.

While it is important to recognize the traits which encourage creativity, it is more important to remember that each of us is born with the ability to create. By understanding the process of creativity, we can enhance our creative abilities.

The Creativity Process

The creativity process has several distinct stages:

Preparation—Gathering information, concentrating and becoming thoroughly familiar with all the aspects of the problem.

Incubation—Taking time out, putting the problem away, letting the mind rest and gather energy.

Illumination—The AHA! When the answer suddenly appears—often when you are completely relaxed and doing something else such as jogging, showering or driving in your car.

Implementation—Solving the practical problems, enlisting the support of other people, locating the necessary resources.

We will concentrate on the preparation and illumination stages. Mindmapping helps us pull information together in such a way that it can bounce around and make new connections. It concentrates our thoughts and information quickly and intensely and often shoots us directly into the illumination stage.

Blocks to Creativity

In order to develop our creative potential, we need to move past mental barriers which prevent us from exploring our creative abilities. The biggest barrier is the voice in our head which continually tells us all the reasons why we can't do something and all the reasons why something won't work.

Eugene Raudsepp, author of the outstanding *Creative Growth Games* series, calls this inner voice

"Mindyapping"

"mindyapping." While this logical inner voice is an important part of our critical judgment, it needs to be suspended during the beginning of the creative process. We need to suspend or delay this judgmental voice and allow our mind to generate lots of possibilities. Many of these possibilities will be discarded later, but by allowing our minds to generate freely without fear of judgment, we will have more possible choices. It is important to remember that we will come back to this logical voice during the implementation stage.

Delay judgment to increase creativity

In our efforts to be constantly logical and rational, we have set up many barriers to creativity. Roger von Oech calls these barriers "mental locks." These locks keep us from being more creative. When we want to be creative we need to be able to break through these barriers.

Here are von Oech's locks from *A Whack on the Side of the Head*:

Avoid these "locks" and increase your creativity

The Right Answer—Most of our lives we are taught to find "the right answer." We get very little practice in generating lots of possible answers. Emile Chartier hit the nail squarely on the head when he said, *"Nothing is more dangerous than an idea when it is the only one you have."*

That's Not Logical—Applying logic too early in the thinking process closes off avenues of thought which might have produced breakthrough ideas if they had been pursued.

Follow the Rules—Rules are important but need to be set aside occasionally to let "unruly" thoughts play around. Picasso said, *"Every act of creation is first of all an act of destruction."*

Be Practical—Being practical implies being judgmental. Early judgment is the death of ideas. The dumbest ideas sometimes get translated into big wins—if they aren't killed too early.

Avoid Ambiguity—When ideas or facts are ambiguous or fuzzy, the mind works harder, probing for new connections or patterns. This process leads to new ideas and discoveries.

To Err Is Wrong—If you are afraid to make mistakes, you will not take chances. Creativity requires a leap into unknown space which often results in failure—you can't bat 1.000 and be creative.

Play Is Frivolous—Messing about with stuff or ideas is a basic part of the creative process.

That's Not My Area—Many great discoveries occurred when someone was "messing around" in a new area.

Don't Be Foolish—Be foolish. Be silly. This foolishness isn't forever—eventually you will put your logical hat back on.

I'm Not Creative—How do you know? You were born creative; your creativity is still there . . . waiting.

Von Oech's books are loaded with fun exercises and thought games to lead you into higher states of creativity. They should be part of the process of developing your creativity skills.

Avoid "expert-itis"

Another major barrier to creativity is "expert-itis": the assumption of knowledge. If we think we know everything about a subject or a problem, we close ourselves off to new input and to new ideas. Daniel Boorstin, librarian of Congress emeritus, says, *"The main obstacle to progress is not ignorance, but the illusion of knowledge."*

Overcoming Rejection:

- Dr. Seuss's first children's book was rejected by 28 publishers.
- In 1971, Dr. Raymond Damadian devised a method of producing body images which were more vivid than X rays. Critics said he was crazy and that his theory of nuclear magnetic resonance was visionary nonsense. Scientific journals refused to publish his works and he could not find funding for his research. Today, scanning equipment using his technology is part of mainstream medicine.
- Harry Warner, of Warner Brothers, said in 1927, "Who the hell wants to hear actors talk?"
- Twenty-one major corporations turned down Chester Carlson's vision of xerography, the technological foundation of Xerox Corporation.
- Albert Einstein said in 1932, "There is not the slightest indication that nuclear energy will ever be obtainable. It would mean that the atom would have to be shattered at will."

Treat failure and rejection as just information

Everyone faces rejection at some stage of his journey. Rejection can come because others do not recognize the value of what you are doing or it can come because you're wrong. What matters is that you learn to accept the rejection as just another piece of feedback . . . another bit of data. And go on. Think about a child learning to walk. If falling down was interpreted as failure, none of us would ever walk. Learning to deal with failure, rejection and frustration is a critical part of the creative process. As we learn to accept these attitudes and move on, we become stronger and more confident.

What's the worst that can happen?

The worst result of rejection is when it stops us from taking action. It can stop the creative process. One technique for handling this rejection is to think of the worst possible thing that could happen to you if you or your idea is rejected. Could they hang you? Draw and quarter you? Take away your children? Pour molten lava over your head? Use humor to think of all the things that probably won't happen if you're rejected. You will usually come down to—"All they can do is say, 'No.' " No is not a killer word. It can inform us; it can redirect us; but we should not let it stop us.

We desperately need more creativity and innovation in our businesses, in our families, in our country and in the world. The ability to innovate will make the difference between success and failure in almost every situation where it is applied. Matthew Holtzberg who invented the plastic passenger car engine (which weighs 200 pounds less than the same engine designed with metal) said in an interview reported in *Vital Speeches of the Day*, *"If we lose our imagination then we lose our ability to progress and evolve. Basically, every new idea is a dream, is a thought."*

For Me to Be More Creative, I Am Waiting For . . .

David Campbell, Ph.D., of the Center for Creative Leadership, gives us a rather humorous list of reasons for waiting to be creative. Here are just a few: *I am waiting for . . .*

- Inspiration
- Permission
- My youth to return
- The two minute warning
- The coffee to be ready
- More time
- The kids to leave home
- My ego to improve
- A signal from Heaven
- Next season
- My ship to come in
- A better deodorant
- Less risk
- Shorter lift lines
- A less turbulent time
- Jacks or better

What are you waiting for? Do any of these reasons sound familiar? Here is an invitation to you to stop waiting and to get in touch with your creativity. Have fun and enjoy your creativity!

Exercises:

1. *The Shining* by Theron Raines is a wonderful, short tale about three Martian men who come to earth and make their entrance by crashing through the skylight of the Metropolitan Museum of Art.

Imagine that you have just crash landed in your living room after the long journey from Mars—What would you see? How would you describe the things around you? Try to comprehend the knowledge base it takes to just identify your surroundings.

2. Look at any object around you and ask Why? Why does it function that way? Why is it built

that way? Why is it that color or shape? Ask yourself . . .

- **Why does a chair have legs?**
- **Why are mountains purple at dusk?**
- **Why is there sand?**
- **Why are apples red and oranges orange?**
- **Why are buildings square?**
- **Why do cars have four wheels?**

3. Don Campbell, music teacher, has his students tell their troubles to a bowl of yellow Jell-O. "It's like a Zen koan. You just can't think in an ordinary way when you're talking to a bowl of Jell-O. Getting the brain unstuck from its old ways of communicating—that's the key to enhancing creative power." (From *Thinking About Thinking* by Clark McKowen.)

Talk to a bowl of Jell-O (even if you have to imagine it). Tell it your troubles.

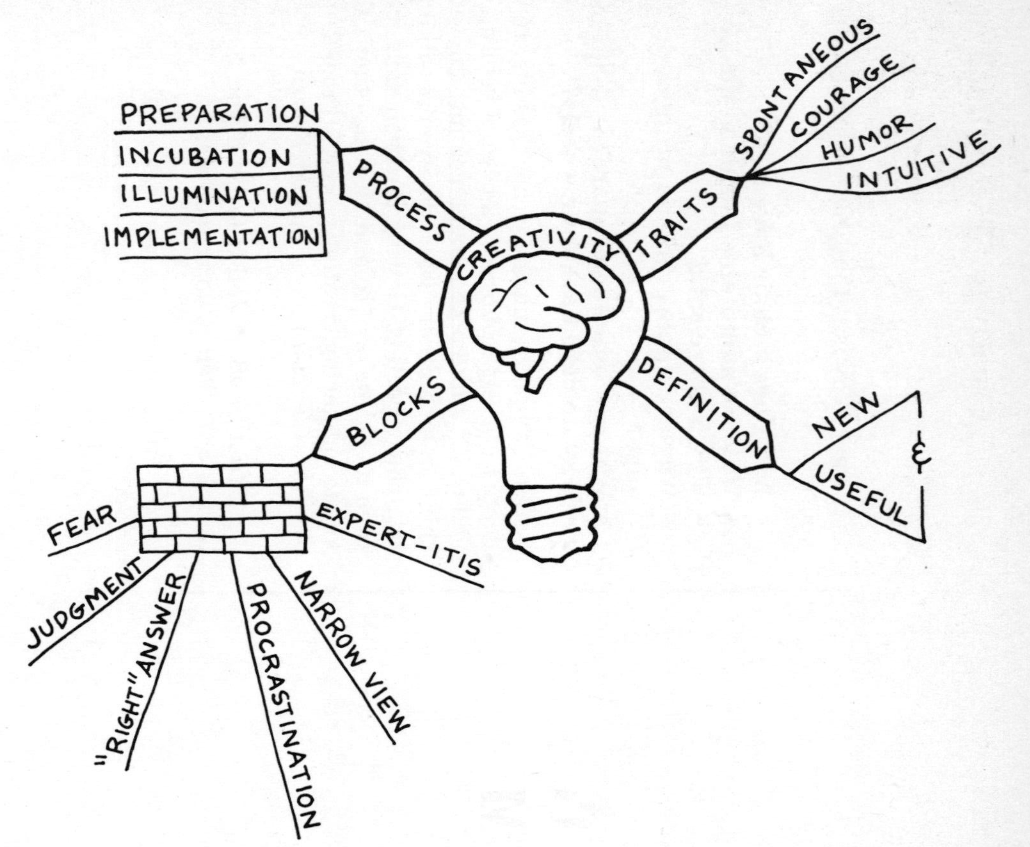
CREATIVITY
PROCESS
PREPARATION
INCUBATION
ILLUMINATION
IMPLEMENTATION
TRAITS
SPONTANEOUS
COURAGE
HUMOR
INTUITIVE
DEFINITION
NEW
&
USEFUL
BLOCKS
FEAR
JUDGMENT
"RIGHT" ANSWER
PROCRASTINATION
NARROW VIEW
EXPERT-ITIS

SECTION TWO

Techniques of Mindmapping

Car Seats
High chairs
Play pens
Baby Beds
Potty, [illegible]
Baby Swing
Stroller
Walkers
Musical boxes

Wagons
Bike, helmets, knee pads
Hot wheel type
Gyms
Monitors
Humidifiers
table tennis
Golf clubs
tennis rackets

Skates
Skooters
Youth beds!
Bassinet
newborn package
Building Blocks

Suggested videos, tapes CD's
Grandparents House
Fun Book
Playhouse

Chapter 3: Mindmapping: Whole Brain Thinking Technique

In the new forms of education, the previous emphasis must be reversed. Instead of first teaching the individual facts about other things, we must first teach him facts about himself—facts about how he can learn, think, recall, create, and solve problems.
—Tony Buzan

Tony Buzan, the developer of mindmapping, once said, "the average business executive has spent between 1,000 and 10,000 hours formally learning economics, history, languages, literature, mathematics and political science. The same executive has spent less than ten hours learning about creative thinking."

Ideas and thoughts flow freely

It was this realization that led him into the development of mindmapping, one of the most effective skills in the process of creative thinking. Mindmapping is a whole brain, visually interesting version of outlining. It has none of the constraints of outlining—you don't have to follow a strict format of Roman numerals, capital letters, numbers, etc. Because mindmapping is not restrictive, your mind allows information to flow more freely. The information also organizes itself into clusters as it flows from the mind to the page.

5 to 7 minute "mind bursts"

Recent brain/mind research has shown that the mind's attention span is extremely short—between five and seven minutes depending upon subject matter and level of interest. The mind works best in these short bursts of activity. Mindmapping takes advantage of the tendency of the mind to work in short, intense "mind bursts" by allowing you to "dump" your ideas and thoughts onto paper in just a few minutes.

Pinball thinking: keeping information "in play"

Mindmapping also allows your mind to explore patterns. Think of a pinball machine. The steel ball rolls through the playing field bouncing off rubber barriers, lighting lights, setting off bells, jumping out of holes, racking up points with each move. A skillful player will be able to flip the ball back into play when it approaches home and thus start the ball through the playing field scoring more and more points. The longer the ball is kept in play, the higher the point count. The mind is similar in that the longer we keep information in play, the more opportunity that information has to make new connections, to bounce off other ideas and information and to score new ideas. It is easy and safe to let the idea roll home into the first normal connection, but it doesn't produce much of a score.

Mindmapping Applications

Mindmapping has an almost unlimited number of uses—any process which requires information or organization can benefit from this technique. Here are a few of the uses which will be discussed in the following chapters:

Writing—Whether you are organizing material for a report for work or exploring a character for a new novel, mindmapping will help you bring depth and richness to your writing. Because it allows you to get into the material so quickly, it helps break writer's block and get your writing project flowing.

Project Organization—Mindmapping is an excellent way to begin "chunking" down a project. You can have a basic structure of any project mapped out in just a few minutes.

Multiple uses

Brainstorming—Individual and group brainstorming sessions respond positively to the free flowing structure of mindmapping.

Meetings—Much of our work time is spent in meetings. Mindmapping gives you a way to make this time more productive.

"To Do" Lists—If standard "to do" lists don't seem to be working for you, try this method.

Presentations—Mindmapping gives you an easy way to prepare for speeches; it helps your audience to understand and remember more of what you are presenting.

Note Taking—This visually interesting method of note taking allows you to organize information as you receive it, add connections and associations and increase the retention of the information.

Personal Growth—Mindmapping taps into our deepest thoughts and provides an effective method of discovering our inner selves.

Mindmapping Elements

The greatest power of mindmapping is that it trains your brain to see the whole picture and the details . . . to integrate logic and imagination.
—Michael Gelb

In the sixties, when Tony Buzan was the editor of the *International Mensa Journal*, he was challenged by the question of whether or not intelligence could be enhanced. He dedicated his research and study to this question and developed several techniques which had amazing results—IQ scores increased, memory improved and thinking skills were enhanced. One of the primary techniques he developed was mindmapping.

Buzan developed mindmapping as a whole brain approach to outlining and note taking. In his book *Use Both Sides of Your Brain*, he emphasizes the use of mindmapping to improve learning and project organization.

In the past several years Buzan and his collaborator, Michael Gelb, have taught this technique to thousands of people through their workshops and books. As it has become more common in schoolrooms and business offices, the number of uses of this amazingly simple, yet powerful, tool have multiplied.

As mindmapping has become more common, other forms of nonlinear note taking have also developed with a variety of names—spider writing, brain webs, clustering and others. And while mindmapping is a form of nonlinear note taking, not all forms of nonlinear note taking are mindmapping. As Buzan was developing and researching this technique, he realized that there were definite benefits gained from each element of mindmapping. These elements are:

Explore all the elements of the mindmapping process

- Central focus of an image or graphic representation of the problem or information being mapped is placed in the center of a page.
- Ideas are allowed to flow freely without judgment.
- Key words are used to represent ideas.
- One key word is printed per line.
- Key word ideas are connected to the central focus with lines.
- Color is used to highlight and emphasize ideas.
- Images and symbols are used to highlight ideas and stimulate the mind to make other connections.

Many of the other forms of nonlinear note taking do not use all of the elements of mindmapping—some of them do not emphasize the central image or the use of colors. Some styles use circles rather than lines. All styles of nonlinear note taking start the mind working in a more free-flowing fashion. The basic forms of nonlinear note taking can help you organize more effectively, write better and enhance your thinking skills. However, on your journey to personal creativity, you will want to explore the more right brain elements of color and images in your mindmapping process.

Since many people are intimidated by the idea of drawing pictures and using colors, this book is organized in a progressive fashion. You will first learn basic nonlinear note taking and then add color and images to progress into mindmapping.

I discovered mindmapping early in 1980. My background was finance and accounting, and I was a very logical, nonvisual person. The first mindmaps I saw were intimidating because they contained lots of color and pictures, and they looked unorganized and somehow "unprofessional." After playing with the technique a few times, however, I discovered what a powerful tool it was and started using it consistently. Gradually, I started adding more color, more symbols and occasionally images. My mindmaps still aren't very artistic, but they help me think more creatively, organize information more easily and manage projects better.

Mindmapping allows you to get information down on paper the way your mind handles it rather than in a rigid outline form. Each mindmap is a unique product of the person who produces it—there are no right or wrong mindmaps . . . no rigid outline forms. Mindmaps are not an end product. No one is ever going to buy your mindmaps. It is simply a technique to help you get your ideas down on paper, to make new connections in your thinking, to organize projects quickly and efficiently and to become more creative.

(After writing the above paragraph, Michael Gelb informed me that one of his and Buzan's students did a mindmap that was so beautiful it was sold to an art dealer who had 1,000 posters made from it!)

Mindmapping allows your mind to dump its information on paper. It encourages you to make associations and to look for new paths of thinking. It delays the critical, judgmental part of the thinking process. Although judgment is an essential part of innovation and creativity, it kills the creative, generative part of the process if applied too early. When we begin to think about a problem or a situation, we want our thoughts to flow and ramble. We want every association, every connection, every pattern to come out so we can pick and choose what works best.

Getting Started

To begin mindmapping, you only need to have a piece of paper and something to write with. As we get further into mindmapping, we will talk about how to get better mindmaps and thoughts by using color, images and different types of paper and pens. For now, though, any paper and pen will do.

Select your focus carefully

In a box in the center of your paper, print the focus of your thinking. This should be one or two words which capture the essence of the problem or situation that you want to think about. Defining the focus of your situation guides the outcome of your thinking, so this step should be done carefully.

Before committing to your focus, you may want to define the elements of your situation. For example: If you are a supervisor with the problem of having a tardy employee, you might put that employee's name in your focus box. However, if you do, your thoughts will circle around that employee rather than any other elements of the situation. If you define the elements of the situation, you might come up with:

Look at all of the elements of the situation to find your focus

Problem Elements:
Sam, the tardy employee
Tardiness in general
The work schedule
Your expectations
Personnel policies and procedures
Employee morale
Employee productivity

By giving yourself a chance to review the elements, you may pick a focus which will lead you through a more productive thought process. You will get a totally different thought process starting with employee productivity than you would have focusing your thoughts on the employee who has the tardiness problem. The process of thinking around a problem or generating different ways of looking at a situation is called divergent thinking. It is important to spend time with the divergent part of the process before beginning to judge and analyze the problem as part of the "convergent" thinking stage.

Allow divergent thinking

Let's assume that once you work through your focus list, you decide that "employee morale" is what you want your focus to be. So the beginning of your mindmap looks like this:

Focus . . . First Step of Mindmapping

Print key words

As your thoughts on employee morale start to pour out, you *print* the *key words* of the thoughts and connect them to the focus with lines. It is critical that you use just key words, because you want to capture your thoughts quickly—you need to capture just enough information to stimulate your memory when you go back later to review.

Key words are nouns and verbs which carry a lot of meaning. Put only one word on a line, as that will allow more associations to be made with that word. Printing is important because it makes more of a visual image in the mind and it will be easier to read when you review later.

As you start to think about employee morale, you might think of problems, causes and possible improvement actions. These would flow out from your focus box:

Associate and connect ideas with lines, arrows, symbols

Let Ideas Flow Out From Center Focus

As ideas are generated which relate to one of these branches, you print the key word and associate it to the branch with a line. New ideas radiate out from the central focus box. When you thought "problems," that might have triggered "tardiness," "low productivity," "increasing use of sick leave." The key words for these thoughts would be connected to the problems branch.

Symbols such as "up arrow" and "down arrow" can be used for modifiers such as high or low. You should develop a series of symbols which are a shorthand way of communicating with yourself. Some common symbols are:

↑ Up arrow—More, higher, increasing
↓ Down arrow—Less, fewer, decreasing
→ Right arrow—Faster
← Left arrow—Slower
!—Excitement, definitely
?—Uncertainty, check later
*—Important idea, or see quote

Because mindmapping is your way to get the most out of your mind, any system which makes sense to you is right.

Writing down ideas gets your mind "unstuck"

As you start to mindmap, allow yourself to put down everything that comes to your mind. Even if something seems totally unrelated, it is important to put it down. If you try to ignore the idea or brush it aside as unimportant, your mind gets stuck on it and it will either keep playing that idea or it will block the flow of other ideas. It's like a record when the needle gets stuck in a track—it plays the same music over and over. Your mind is like that when it rejects an idea.

Two things happen when you allow yourself to put the idea down—the first is that the mind is freed to go onto other ideas, and the second is that associations are made with this idea. Sometimes this is where the best ideas come from. Occasionally you may find yourself going down a completely

Do not judge or edit ideas

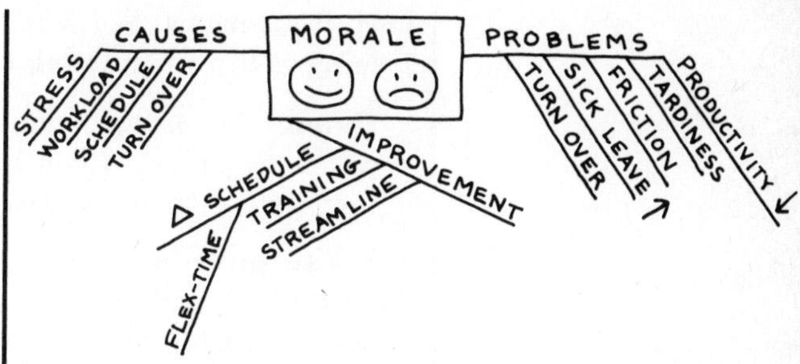

Put Down All of Your Ideas

unrelated path. With mindmapping, these sidepaths seldom last more than a few seconds, and either the path will end and you'll come back to your original focus, or you'll find that the path really did relate and you just couldn't see the relationship at the beginning of the path.

If you remember that mindmapping is not an end result, it's just part of the process, then it's easier to remember that whatever you do on your mindmap is OK. *There are no wrong mindmaps.*

Additional Tips:

Change your "8½-by-11 mentality"

Because so much of our educational process is oriented toward left brain training, anything you can do to encourage your right brain traits will help you generate more ideas. For most of our school and business life, we have written on 8½-by-11-inch paper with a black pen or pencil. You can change this 8½-by-11 mentality by changing the size or color of paper you use and by using different colored pens. Large size computer paper is great for mindmaps. If you don't have anything available other than standard size paper, at least turn it sideways. You will find it amazing how freeing it can be to break out of this rut.

Paper—Try large computer paper, easel paper or poster paper—if you have to use 8½-by-11-inch paper, turn it sideways.

White Boards—White boards and mindmapping were made for each other. Get the biggest board possible and lots of colored markers. Dennison makes portable white board pads called "static images" that are excellent for meetings, seminars and brainstorming sessions. Franklin International sells a portable white board that fits day planning systems. So you never have to be without a white board and a mindmapping surface.

Color and Images—Experiment with different colors. Break the black on white connection, and let your mind play with colors and images. Use colors and images to associate thoughts and make them vivid.

Flow—Keep your hands moving. If your thoughts stop, draw circles or lines until new associations start showing up.

Stand up and do your mindmap on a white board, chalkboard, or poster paper. Listen to music. Write left-handed.

Anything you do that is different from usual will help you make new connections.

Exercises:

Spend no more than five minutes mindmapping one or two of the following words.

- Watch how your mind makes connections and associations.

- Write as fast as you can but be sure to print and use key words.
- Try to print only one word per line.
- Put down every thought.

Wood
Run
Yellow
Music
Desk
Stove

Adding Color, Music and Images

See deep enough and you see musically; the heart of nature being everywhere music if you can only reach it.
—Thomas Carlyle

Black-and-white television was a breakthrough. We were awed by the first fuzzy images on the tiny screen. But our awe was short-lived, and soon we wanted color and sharp, life-sized images.

We go through a similar process when we begin mindmapping. At first, we can make amazing breakthroughs just using a pencil and paper. But soon we start to want more. As we get used to the novelty of the mindmapping technique, we want to experiment with more right brain modes of thinking. This leads us to color, symbols, images and music.

Color Activates the Brain

The world around us is full of color. Through the eons of evolution our brains have developed elaborate mechanisms for perceiving and using color. Studies have shown that color can excite or soothe us. We like color; it is natural and more interesting than an artificial black-and-white world.

Adding color to your mindmaps is a natural progression. Color can be used in several ways.

- **Organization**—You can use colors to highlight different areas of your mindmaps . . . to organize information into separate topic areas.
- **Brainstorming**—After an initial brainstorming session, you may want to go back and use a different color to highlight ideas for further brainstorming or to select key points. Some groups give each participant a different color so they can identify their contributions.
- **Presentations**—Presenting information in color-coded areas increases retention of that information. People will remember that the information was in the "red area" or in the "green area."
- **Idea Flow**—If your energy runs low or your ideas stop while you are mindmapping, changing colors will sometimes start a new channel of thought.

Carlton Wagner, director of the Wagner Institute for Color Research, says that colors are processed in different sequences and the first color processed is yellow. When you want to highlight a key idea or point, highlighting that idea in yellow will make you, or your audience, perceive that point first.

Images and Symbols—Brain Shorthand

Images and symbols are shorthand to the brain. The right side of the brain quickly perceives images and patterns. Adding symbols and images to your mindmaps will help communicate your message visually to your mind or to the mind of your audience. Whenever you can communicate your message in several ways, the chances of that message being received fully will increase.

Music Increases Right Brain Activity

Music also communicates directly with the right brain and turns on that part of our thinking processes. You may want to experiment to see what works best for you. While writing this book, I found Ray Lynch's *Deep Breakfast* was an automatic turn-on for writing. Anytime I was having trouble writing, I would put on the headphones, turn on *Deep Breakfast—loud*—and the writing would start. It worked for me—experiment until you find music that works for you.

Exercises:

Here are some ideas to mindmap:

Light
Friend
Work
Play

Spring
Ring
Cooking
Books

Turn on some background music—classical, new age or other instrumental music which makes you feel good. Then mindmap one of the ideas above.
Try the following techniques:

Images—Draw an image of the idea in the center of the page and let your thoughts radiate from that image.

Whenever you run low on ideas, draw an image of one of the ideas on your map and let that stimulate more thoughts and associations.

Color—Have several colored pens available and change colors when you want to emphasize an idea or to add organization to your thoughts. Play with the colors and see how that influences your thoughts.

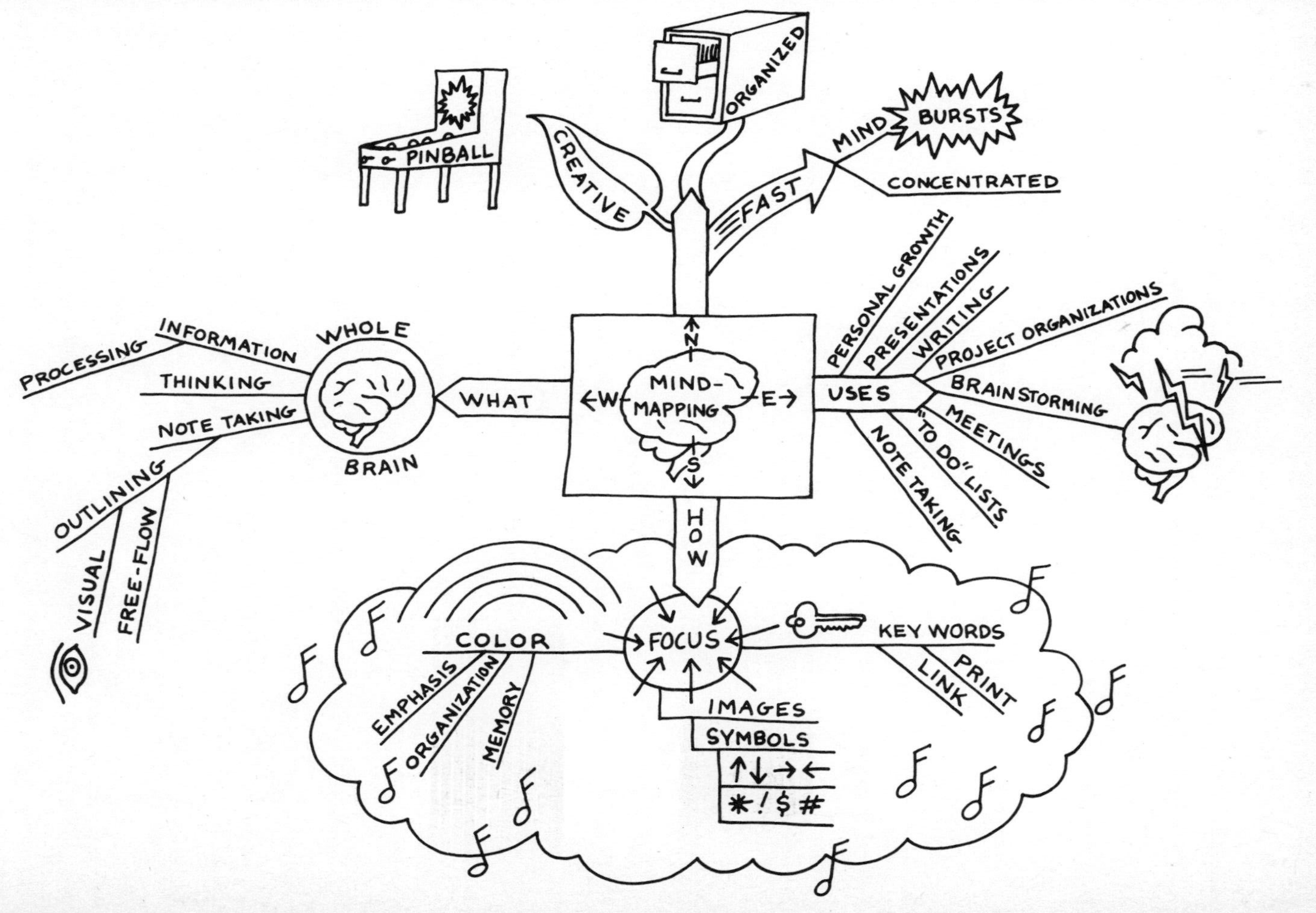

MIND-MAPPING
N
S
E
W
PINBALL
CREATIVE
ORGANIZED
FAST
MIND
BURSTS
CONCENTRATED
USES
PERSONAL GROWTH
PRESENTATIONS
WRITING
PROJECT ORGANIZATIONS
BRAINSTORMING
MEETINGS
"TO DO" LISTS
NOTE TAKING
WHAT
WHOLE
BRAIN
INFORMATION
PROCESSING
THINKING
NOTE TAKING
OUTLINING
VISUAL
FREE-FLOW
HOW
FOCUS
COLOR
EMPHASIS
ORGANIZATION
MEMORY
KEY WORDS
PRINT
LINK
IMAGES
SYMBOLS
↑↓→←
*!$#

SECTION THREE

Applications of Mindmapping

Chapter 4: Writing Can Be Easy, Effortless and Enjoyable

Colors fade, temples crumble, empires fall, but wise words endure.
—Edward Thorndike

Mindmapping is an excellent way to generate and organize ideas before beginning to write. It is an almost guaranteed way to break writer's block. Gabriele Lusser Rico, professor of Creative Arts in English at San Jose State University developed a method of nonlinear note taking for her writing students. She termed this method "clustering" and says, "Through clustering we naturally come up with a multitude of choices from a part of our mind where the experiences of a lifetime mill and mingle. It is the writing tool that accepts wondering, not knowing, seeming chaos, gradually mapping an interior landscape as ideas begin to emerge."

The "aha" is finding your theme

Often the hardest part of writing is knowing what you want to write about . . . what your theme is and how to begin. When you mindmap and allow your ideas and thoughts to radiate out around the page, you will come to a place where you suddenly "know" what you want to write. It is a feeling of "Aha, that's it!" One idea or memory has given you a focus for writing. When you have that feeling, it is easy to begin writing. You are pulled into the writing and writer's block melts away.

Here is an example of a student's clustering of "onion" and the writing that resulted. You can almost feel how the memory of cooking onions triggered a whole image and practically dictated the writing. This student described herself as "not a writer" but the image is so vivid that you can almost touch it.

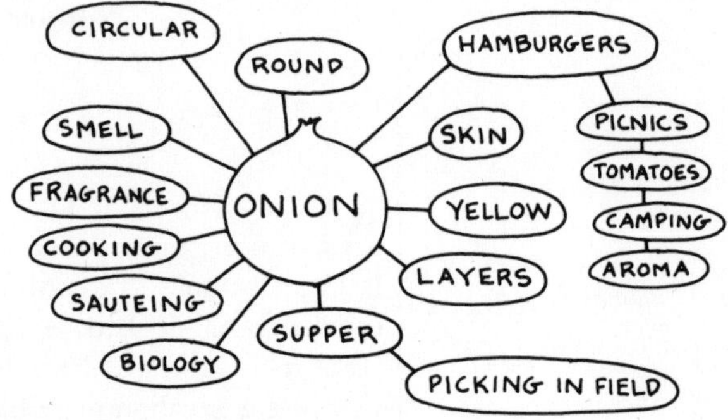

Clustering of "onion"

"I was a small child living in the country. In the late afternoon, I remember laying on my stomach on the seat of our swing and turning around lazily, spinning first one way, then the other, my bare toe making circles in the dirt of the play yard. The hens are making soft cackling noises. Suddenly I hear the screen door slam and my mother calling me for supper. I become attuned to everything and smell the aroma of pork chops and onions."

—Helen Andrewson

Letting Go

The following two writing samples are from students who mindmapped "letting go." Notice the totally different results of the exercise.

> "I remember the fights, the tears, sharing a bed, pulling the blankets. Dad liked me best but you were always the prettiest—the most popular. I was always just your little sister. Ah, but now it is so sweet, the two of us spending time together . . . letting go. Sharing memories, giggling, talking all night, being kids again, setting straight old, confusing feelings. Feeling secure and very loved. What a joy, letting go and spending time with my best friend . . . my sister."
>
> —Terrell Hedstrom

> "I stand before my closet turning hangers this way and that. Being unable to decide should I keep this one or that. There is no more room . . . I have to let go—for there's a new sale at Nordstrom's Rack!"
>
> —Linda Cannon

Mindmapping taps your subconscious mind

Mindmapping allows you to get in touch with your subconscious mind before writing; it helps you produce more emotion, more color, more rhythm. Your writing then reflects more accurately the uniqueness that is you.

The only thing we have to offer in our writing is the sum of our individual experiences filtered through our singular combination of talents, perspective and consciousness. When we allow the truth of our individuality to emerge in our writing, we are expressing our creativity. When we can express our individuality so that it touches a responsive chord in others, we have reached creative communication.

Write . . . write to others, write to yourself

In order to develop your creative writing skills, you should take every opportunity to write. Write letters to friends describing events in your life. Pick a subject you care about and write little essays to yourself. When you see a person who interests you, take a few minutes and draw a word picture of the person. Jot your thoughts down in a notebook—even if it's just a description of a sunset, a flower or how your heart felt when your boss yelled at you.

Just like every other skill, writing takes exercise and the exercise of writing is writing. However, it is also the process of discovering your mind. Just as painting is a translation into color, form and line of the artist's mind, writing is the translation into words, rhythm and structure of the writer's mind. You should become familiar with how your mind operates—not in an analytical way, but in order to better understand its processes.

Mindmapping: discovery tool

Mindmapping helps you discover your mind. Your mind is the universe . . . your universe. Exploring it has all the excitement, all the joy and wonder of exploring the world around you. Since most subjects take just a few minutes to mindmap, you should practice this skill often. Take any word that strikes you and use it as your focus. Mindmap that word for a few minutes, putting down all connections even if they don't seem particularly relevant. When you reach the "aha" point, write a few sentences until you have the basic idea of what you wanted to communicate.

Exercise:

Here are a few words which might trigger interesting mindmaps and writing. Take any of these ideas, mindmap it for a few minutes and then write a short paragraph about the subject. These are especially good as a warm-up exercise to get your mind started before going on to a writing project.

Neutral warm-ups

Letting go
My favorite teacher
Duty
Checkerboard
Measles
Puppy
Autumn
Church
Poison
Erotic
Shoes
Caboose
My special place
Stress
Scarlet
Firefly
Poinsetta
Shrimp
Valentine
Ruby
Pink elephants
Green
Blood
Santa Claus

Remember:

- Print key word associations and connect with lines to the central focus.
- Print all associations that come to your mind—do not judge your thoughts.
- Allow those associations to trigger new associations.
- Relate the associations to each other with lines.

- When you have reached an "aha" or your energy has stopped, write a few sentences.

These are just exercises, but you may want to keep them in a notebook so that you can track your thinking processes.

Mindmapping is playful—powerful play—and our mind responds to the fun and playfulness. Because it is playful, joyful, colorful and full of imagery, mindmapping encourages the brain of the mapper. It turns it on—energizes it.

Business Writing . . . Putting Yourself Ahead of the Pack

As soon as you move one step up from the bottom, your effectiveness depends on your ability to reach others through the spoken or written word.
—Peter Drucker

Poor writing skills handicap your career

Writing abilities are as visible as a person's wardrobe. Impressions may last even longer, as files containing written work are read and reread. You may be bright, ambitious and hardworking (upright, loyal and trustworthy) and yet have a handicap which will stall your career climb on the lower rungs of the ladder: poor writing skills. You can persuade, direct and influence the course of your organization and the direction of your career through thoughtful, well-organized memos and reports.

This does not mean that you have to be able to write like Hemingway in order to be successful. It does mean that you should be able to write what you mean in a way that the person you are writing to will read and understand it the way you mean it. It does mean that your written work should look clean and "well dressed" and that it should be organized and coherent.

Red Smith said, *"There's nothing to writing. All you do is sit down at a typewriter and open a vein."* But, it doesn't have to be *that* difficult.

Here are three easy steps guaranteed to improve your writing:

Listen . . . Organize . . . Telegraph

LOT System

That sounds overly simplistic—and it is. However, if you remember and practice the LOT system and the tips and techniques gathered here, your writing will become a powerful tool . . . one which can set you apart from the pack.

Step One: Listen

A good listener is not only popular everywhere, but after a while, he gets to know something.
—Wilson Mizner

Writing any type of business report or memo should never begin until we have listened carefully to the people involved with the problem. Business writing is part of the problem-solving system: we want to get information, give information, report conclusions, set policy or direct actions. Problem solving begins with listening, and as Gerry Mitchell, chairman of Dana Corporation, states, *"In general, American management is no goddam good at talking to people and listening."*

How much time do we spend during the day actually listening instead of talking? Probably not much, definitely not as much as we should. The communication process has two sides—the initiator, or speaker, and the receiver, or listener. If either piece is missing, there is no communication.

Some guidelines to better listening are:

Listening guidelines

- **Learn to tolerate silence.** We are often intimidated by silence and try to fill the gap. But while we are covering an awkward silence, we may be missing an opportunity to hear what the other person is trying to say.
- **Ask Questions.** Probing, open-ended questions give the speaker a chance to open up and reveal issues and information which would not come out otherwise.
- **Be positive and reinforcing.** The speaker will be more relaxed and open if she feels that you are in sympathy with the discussion and the points being made.
- **Avoid judgments.** Judgments close off conversation. Even if you are opposed to what is being said, if you can keep an open mind, you will hear more than if you let your judgment be known immediately.

Listen to the people close to the problem

Who should you listen to? Not just to the experts—they tend to represent, and defend, the status quo. Listen to the people who are involved with the problem—the people who do the work, the people who work directly with customers, the people who handle complaints. Ross Perot says, *"My first message is: Listen, listen, listen to the people who do the work."* If you want to get a new slant on a situation, you have to find a new perspective, talk to new people, come at it from a different angle.

Writing can be only as good as the thinking that precedes it.
Thinking is only as good as the writing that explains it.

Step Two: Organize

Quick "mind dump"

Once you have gathered information and feel that you have a grasp of the situation, it is time to start organizing the material for writing. This is a perfect place for mindmapping, the whole brain organization method. Mindmapping pulls together all of your ideas, memories, associations and connections in a quick "mind dump." Mindmapping gives you a chance to explore the information creatively, making new connections and organizing the information into its primary pieces or branches and the appropriate subtopics and details.

Focus
Focus
Focus
Focus

A primary result of the mindmapping process should be the **FOCUS**. Focus in a business report or memo is your objective—it is the "why" of why you're bothering to write at all. Focus is as important in writing as it is in photography. Focus separates the pro from the pack of amateurs. Most business writing is unfocused—it doesn't have a goal, a desired end result. It doesn't call for action from the reader. Before turning on your word-processor, answer the following questions:

- Who is my audience?
- What do I want them to do?
- What reasons will they have for not wanting to do what I want them to do?

- What might stop the reader from doing what I suggest?
- Will someone else make the decision?
- Whose ox will this gore? (What are the politics?)

Before beginning to write anything, you should be able to complete this sentence: I want (WHO) to do (WHAT) because (REASON). If you can't write that sentence, you are not ready to start writing. If you can write it, you are ready to decide on strategy.

Know Your Audience

It is important to know who your audience is and how they are likely to perceive your message. If you have empathy with your audience, you will be able to hear with their ears. Excellent writers are generally excellent listeners. They listen carefully to their audience, and they understand how to write in a way that will be well received by their audience. A quick way to lose an audience is to be condescending. Avoid phrases like "As you can clearly see" (How do you know I can?) and "I am sure you will agree" (Why are you so sure?) and "It should be evident" (It should be but . . .).

Knowing your audience will help you organize your material so that it has the best chance of being heard and understood.

Step Three: Telegraph

Decision #1: Do you really need to write this memo or report? If you can do it orally, you are probably better off. ATI Medical, Inc. (150 employees, $14 million sales) abolished memos and only occasionally writes PAPCOES (reverse acronym for "enunciations of corporate policies and procedures"). President Paul Stevenson states, *"Everyone has learned to talk to each other."* Talking to people has wonderful advantages over writing: you get immediate feedback; you strengthen your social contacts; and you save trees.

Don't write it when you can say it

Eliminating written communication probably is not practical or even desirable for most organizations. Whenever possible, however, talk to people and save your written communications for complex issues requiring extensive explanation or documentation.

3 Maxims of Business Writing

There are three principles we must keep in mind when we are doing business writing:

Remember these!

First and foremost:	No one wants to read it!
Second and important:	Almost no one will read all of it!
Third and critical:	Almost everyone will misunderstand some part of it!

We aren't writing the Great American Novel. Instead of entertaining our readers, we are asking them to do something, to make decisions, to add to their already overcrowded schedule. And the first thing we're asking is for them to read what we have written. So we start out, "Per your request, please find enclosed the report on the possible involvement of management in a . . ." Yawn. Z-z-z-z.

You are competing for the time of busy people. Unless you are the chairman of the board or president, you probably have about 30 seconds to grab the interest of your reader. Otherwise you will wind up in the "To Read" file. (And we all know how often we read our "To Read" file!)

Grab attention in 30 seconds!

We need to employ the tools of the advertising folks—headlines; subheads; bullets; short, crisp, active words; visuals; powerful persuasion and dynamic delivery. We need to telegraph our message. We need to grab attention and present our message as powerfully as possible.

Mindmapping helps us organize our information and telegraph our message. It clarifies our focus and concentrates on short, active key words. Here are some quick guidelines to help you put your written materials in a sharp, concise, powerful package.

Headlines Should Pack Meaning

Don't waste headlines

Headlines are golden—don't waste them. A report headline might read "Summary of Benefits" or "Three Million in Savings." Which would grab your attention?

Writing order:

1. **Headlines**
2. **Visuals**
3. **Subheads**
4. **Body**

If you use headlines and subheads wisely, you can telegraph most of your information to even the most cursory reader—and, remember, almost no one will read everything you have written. One way to write a report is to start with the headlines, then go to the graphics and subheads and, after those are perfected, write the in-between stuff. This procedure keeps your **FOCUS** in mind and prevents you from following a distracting tangent.

Visuals Sell Your Message

Visuals communicate instantly

Pictures, graphs or illustrations are very important when you are trying to get an idea across quickly or emphasize a particular point. An effective graph or picture can persuade in an instant. But there are some things to keep in mind:

- Graphs and charts have more impact than tables.

One idea per picture or graph

- Each graph, chart or picture should make only one point. Better to have several graphs, each making one point than one confusing graph with little impact.
- Add color if at all possible.
- Keep the graph or picture as close to the related text as possible.

Short Is Best

Short but not childish

Short words . . . short sentences . . . short paragraphs. The trick is to write them without sounding like a second-grade primer. Short words do not have to be dull. They can be crisp, punchy, colorful, musical, poetic and graphic. They can lift, stomp, drag, kick and breathe life into your work. Short sentences are active and quickly understood.

Jargon and Acronyms Can Be Useful or Deadly

Jargon is shorthand . . . useful but tricky

Every profession has its terminology, acronyms and jargon. When everyone understands the terms, it provides a quick and efficient shorthand. It's almost impossible to avoid jargon and acronyms, and when you are writing for in-house people, you're probably pretty safe. But, you are always safe when you define an acronym or technical term at least the first time in a paper.

Format Should Fit the Function

The format of what you're writing should fit its function. If you receive a memo and your response is a short note or decision, you may want to just jot your response on the memo and send it back. But if you are responsible for presenting an analysis of a new market, you will want a formal report complete with charts, graphs and documentation. Making the format fit the function of your writing seems simple, but, all too often, a brief request triggers a three-page memo. The hierarchy of format should be reviewed to make sure your response fits the requirements—you should not move up the hierarchy unless the situation requires it.

Communication hierarchy

Verbal—informal, no documentation

Handwritten—informal, documentation required

Memos—broad communication required (more than three people) and documentation required

Reports—broad communication required, complex issues require supporting documentation, decision needs to be documented

Memos

Memos—1 page

Memos should be short (one page for most); use every possible trick for quick communication:

- Headlines
- Short paragraphs
- Bullets
- Modified outline format

A preferred memo heading is:

Date:

TO:
FROM:
SUBJECT:

ACTION REQUIRED:

ACTION REQUIRED: reinforces action request

The "ACTION REQUIRED" line makes the writer think through the purpose of the memo. If there are too many "Info Only" memos, it's time to rethink. It also makes it clear to the reader that the writer expects an action.

Avoid Sexism

A recent study of 500 college students (50% male and 50% female) showed that when they read a story using he, him or his *where the subject could be male or female*, 65% of the study group assumed the subject was male. Recently, people have been sensitized to sexism in writing; therefore, you should avoid sexism whenever possible. However, using awkward constructions such as he/she or (s)he can break the flow of your writing and lessen readability.

Here are some ways to avoid sexism without sacrificing readability:

Tips for avoiding sexism

- Specify the person you are discussing.
- Use plurals. For example:
  A manager should listen to his staff.
  Managers should listen to their staffs.
- Use she sometimes, especially when discussing people of power.
  A president should use her power to . . .
- Substitute less offensive words: person for man; synthetic for man-made; representative for spokesman; worker for workman; labor hours for man hours.

Humor

Use humor sparingly

Humor can be effective in informal writing. However, unless you are positive that the humor will not give offense, it is probably better not to use it. If you are a boss writing to your staff, humor directed at yourself can establish a warm, human tone. If you are an underling, humor directed at yourself might be perceived as lack of self-confidence or weakness.

Even if you are extremely good at humor, you should limit it in your writing. People will come to expect it and your serious communications will be more difficult.

Readability, Please

Here are some housekeeping tips for making your memos and reports more readable:

- **Wide margins**—It is easier to read narrow columns than wide lines. Wide margins also make it easy for the reader to make notes as she reads. It makes the page look clean and professional.
- **Limit upper case**—We normally read upper and lower case text. Putting several lines in all upper case makes those lines difficult to read. Use boldface, italics, or underlining instead.

Make it easy to read

- **Numbers** should be written in a way that makes them easy to read. $4 million is easier than $4,000,000.
- **Page numbers** are mandatory for reports of more than three pages. Trying to discuss unnumbered pages of a report has ruined many meetings.
- **Hyphens** help even out spacing but they do not help readability. Avoid them if you can. If you can't avoid them, review them to make sure they don't stop the flow.
- **Right justification** is popular. Because it's used in newspapers and magazines, we think it looks "professional." However, they use it because it packs more words into a smaller space and saves paper. The uneven spaces make reading more difficult. Avoid when possible.

Revise, Edit, Revise

Revision . . . the professional difference

No one . . . no one . . . writes without revision. To write any memo or report without revising and editing is equivalent to professional Russian roulette. It is almost a given that any error in an important report will be in the most critical place. The president's name will be misspelled; the column of numbers which is the basis of your entire report will not add up. For important communications, have someone else review it. If at all possible let an important report sit for a few days before releasing it. (If you've ever done it, you know how much a few days of rest can improve perspective.)

Read out loud

Review grammar and punctuation questions in a good style manual. If you have a spelling checker, use it. Read your report out loud to catch awkward phrases or passages that sound harsh or unfriendly.

Endings Should Reinforce the Message

Endings summarize and repeat call for action

Endings should provide a sense of closure, summarize the important points and call for the next action to be taken. It is here that many writers leave the reader hanging, not knowing quite what to do next. Make sure you have clearly asked for the action you want.

Words are, of course, the most powerful drug used by mankind.
—Rudyard Kipling

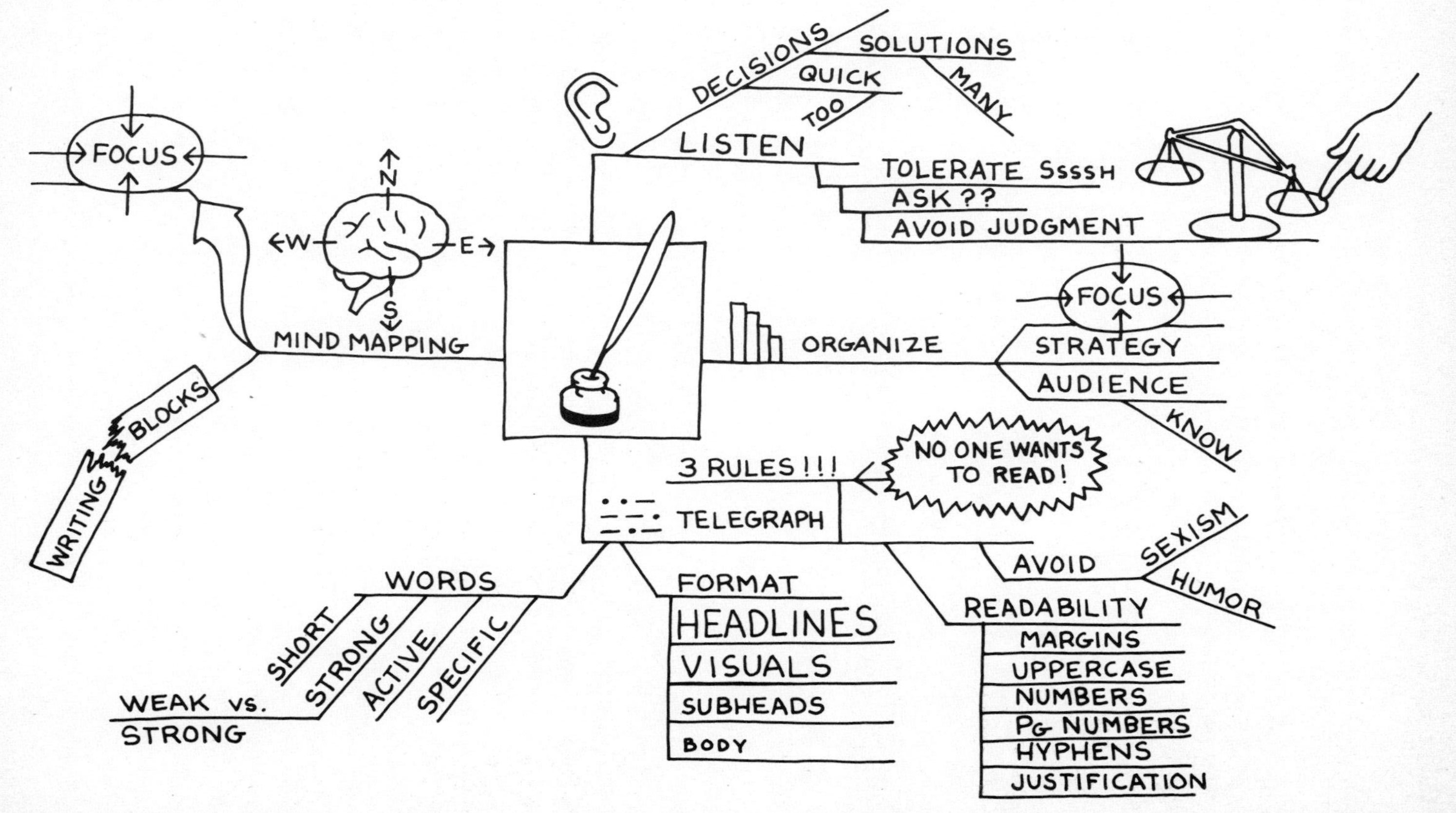
FOCUS
N
W
E
S
MIND MAPPING
WRITING
BLOCKS
LISTEN
DECISIONS
SOLUTIONS
QUICK
TOO
MANY
TOLERATE Ssssh
ASK ??
AVOID JUDGMENT
ORGANIZE
FOCUS
STRATEGY
AUDIENCE
KNOW
3 RULES !!!
NO ONE WANTS TO READ!
TELEGRAPH
AVOID
SEXISM
HUMOR
READABILITY
MARGINS
UPPERCASE
NUMBERS
PG NUMBERS
HYPHENS
JUSTIFICATION
FORMAT
HEADLINES
VISUALS
SUBHEADS
BODY
WORDS
SHORT
STRONG
ACTIVE
SPECIFIC
WEAK vs.
STRONG

Chapter 5: Better Project Management

Business is like riding a bicycle.
Either you keep moving or you fall down.
—John David Wright

Your boss just called you and said he wants to talk about a strategy for winning the Johnson account. You haven't thought about this account because you thought the competition had it locked up. When you get to your boss's office, his secretary tells you he just took a call and will be about five minutes. Do you

a. Read the latest *Business Week* lying in front of you?
b. Try to remember everything you know about Johnson?
c. Talk to the secretary?
d. Mindmap a Johnson account strategy?

All of the choices have potential benefits, but one will have you prepared to discuss strategy and ready to take on a demanding project. If you chose (d), wealth, promotions, fame and fortune await you.

You can use those five minutes to mindmap Johnson's situation: his problems, his needs and the important factors in his market. As you are mapping this background, ideas will automatically start to form on how to approach the account.

Five Minutes to Organization

We tend to throw five minute segments of time away, dismissing them as too trivial to be effective. And yet five minutes is about the average duration of a "mind burst." In five minutes, you can have your thinking about a project started and down on paper. This hardly means you're through, but starting a project is almost as important as finishing it. As Woody Allen says, "80 percent of success is showing up." With mindmapping you can painlessly begin a project and be well on your way to implementation before you've built up "project resistance."

Breaking "project resistance"

You probably know about "project resistance." It's when you avoid a project because it's too hard, too time-consuming, too expensive, too important, too overwhelming, etc. It starts to feel like a huge, black bear lurking on the outskirts of your mind.

You know you're in "project resistance" when you don't start a project because you "don't have enough time." Mindmapping simplifies, organizes and drains away the resistance.

Old Joke: How do you eat an elephant?
Answer: One bite at a time.

WWWWWWH$

WWWWWH$

Mindmapping gives you a tool to take one bite at a time . . . a way of "chunking down" the project. As you break up a project into smaller and smaller chunks, they start to become manageable and the resistance disappears.

Project organization with mindmapping is just like the mindmapping we have seen before with one modification:

> **After you write your focal idea in a box or circle in the middle of the page, write WWWWWH$ in the upper left corner.**

WWWWWH$ stands for Who, What, When, Where, Why, How and Money. As you are mindmapping and come to a hesitation, ask yourself these questions:

Who—Who needs to be involved? Who has information I need? Who will do the tasks? Who will make the decision? Who can put up roadblocks? Who will gain? Who will lose?

What—What do I need to do? What do I need to know? What resources do I have? What resources do I lack? What will the final product look like?

When—When does it need to be done? When does each piece need to happen? How long does it take to get resources?

Where—Where will it happen? Where will I find resources? Where will we be when it happens?

Why—Why does this problem exist? Why is it

important to solve it? Why would anyone pay to have this project done?

How—How should the project be done? How will I know if I have succeeded? How will I find the resources? How will I communicate with others?

Money—What will it cost? Where will the money come from? What will the cost-benefit be?

Mindmapping a summer vacation

As you answer these questions, you use the answers to stimulate new associations, ideas and connections.

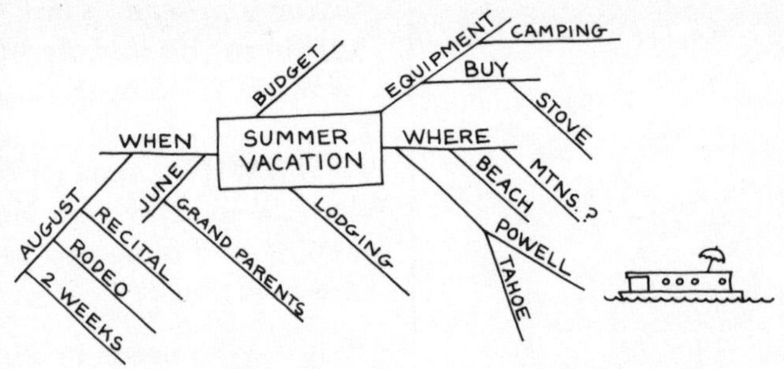

Your mindmap will be an overview of your project and will lead to standard project management techniques such as: to do lists, task assignments, time lines, cost-benefit analysis, etc. Mindmapping is not a replacement for any of these valuable analytical tools. It is a way of looking at a project from above and making sure you have the broad picture before getting inundated with the details.

Organize and Implement Group Projects

Mindmapping is an excellent way to organize and implement projects in a group setting. Its non-hierarchical nature fits the way information flows

Information flows from interested party to interested party

in today's organizations. Rather than top to bottom or bottom to top, information tends to be passed from interested party to interested party, regardless of where they are on a formal organization chart. It spreads out . . . sometimes oozing slowly and sometimes raging wildly. Mindmapping allows people with ideas and information to be productive without going through the "chain of command."

The free-flowing form of the mindmaps, and the way they flow into other maps, makes them perfect for group planning. An easy way to get the group going is to start the project planning on easel paper taped to the wall. Small groups can take branches and make their own maps of the subprojects. This goes on until the project is planned down to assignments and due dates. The visibility and unstructuredness of the maps encourages people to get involved with the maps, making suggestions, changes and corrections without worrying about formality.

A perfect example of the use of this technique happened during the opening of a Sheraton Hotel in Long Beach. Opening a major hotel is a nightmare of logistics. In one very short period of time, a new building comes together with a new management team, new employees, new vendors and new guests. Six weeks before the 400-room Sheraton Long Beach was scheduled to open, senior management decided to get the management team together for two days of training. Their goal was to build teamwork and to develop a strategy which would insure a smooth opening.

The two-day retreat was designed and coordinated by Charlene Walter, director of training, and Jesse Stewart, director of human resources. They had games, toys, music and exercises carefully coordinated to build camaraderie among the 40 managers, most of whom had been part of the team for only a few days. They set goals, discussed values and learned a lot about each other. They also discovered mindmapping.

Team mindmapping

After the retreat, mindmaps started sprouting all over the corporate offices. The myriad of details required to open the hotel became branches of the map. The maps were taped to the walls, and people would get together and add to the maps, cross off items as they were accomplished and create totally new maps as new tasks came up. The process was free-flowing and participatory. There was a sense of adventure and togetherness in the project.

The Sheraton Long Beach opened on schedule. Several of the senior managers, who had been through many openings, commented that this opening was one of the most efficient they had been through. While mindmapping was only a small part of a large effort, it helped promote the type of teamwork and commitment that leads to success in a major project.

The Franklin International Institute in Salt Lake City produces a day planner and teaches time management and project management to corporations, schools, organizations and individuals. They have incorporated mindmapping as a basic skill in their project management courses. Lynne Snead, the head of the project management division, tells a story about how mindmapping allowed a small group to achieve almost unbelievable results on a recent project. Lynne's boss gave her an assignment of developing a student planner—a completely new system to be used by students. This meant understanding how students would use the planner, what they needed to track, what type of forms they would need and what the best structure would be.

As Lynne tells the story, she thought it sounded like an interesting project until she was told that the pilot product needed to be in the store in four-and-a-half months and that a prototype was needed in one week! Fortunately she was asked what resources she needed to meet these goals. She took two staff members (both mindmappers), computers, lots of easel paper and headed off-site for five days. "The first thing we did was to mind-map our goals. We spent about an hour working out a complete map of what we wanted this project to accomplish. That was probably the best time we spent, because in the next few days, whenever a question came up, we would refer back to our goal map to see how it fit in with our objectives."

After determining their goals, the group mind-mapped the sections of the planner. They worked out the structure of what they wanted in the planner and what they wanted each form to do. Mind-maps covered the room as the sections became subsections and the subsections became details. At the end of the five days they not only presented a laser-printed prototype of the planner, but a complete plan as to how the product could be produced and in the store at the scheduled date. The board of directors accepted the plan, and four-and-a-half months later the project was delivered on schedule.

Exercises:

Practice your ability to mindmap a project by spending a few minutes with these exercises. Even though these exercises are all logical, left brain type projects, it is important to remember the basics of mindmapping:

- Allow free-flowing associations.
- Put down everything that comes to your mind even though it may seem useless.
- Print key word ideas—one word per line.
- Connect your associations with lines, arrows, etc.

1. You want to plan a very special, very romantic dinner for your significant other. Mindmap this special occasion.

2. Mindmap your dream vacation. Assume no limitations—time, money, companions and physical abilities are all without limit.

3. Take a project from work that you have been putting off and mindmap it for just five minutes. Set the timer so you don't go over the time limit.

What did you notice about the process? Was it easy . . . fast? Did you have any unexpected associations or thoughts?

Do you feel that you got something out of your five-minute work project?

Mindmapping Your Goals

If you always do what you've always done, you'll always be what you've always been.

Everyone has goals. Our goals direct our actions and our actions take us to our goals. So wherever we are, we are here because our goals and actions led us here. From the presidential candidate whose campaign is an orchestrated schedule of speeches, appearances, endorsements, ads and debates, to the street person hustling quarters for the next meal, our goals (in one case the White House and in the other a fast-food haven) dictate our actions.

Goals direct our actions

We can either direct this process of goals and actions to lead us to where we really want to go, or we can just drift along unfocused. Without direction, we may want to work on a new project one minute, go to the beach the next, or think about calling a friend, or making love, and behind it all have a nagging feeling that we'd like to eat a bagel. In order to survive, we develop methods for bringing order to this chaos so that we're following a general path. However, unless we stop once in a while to analyze and evaluate our goals, we may find that we're on the path to Brooklyn when we wanted to go to Seattle.

Mindmapping your goals opens up new possibilities

Mindmapping provides an excellent technique for reviewing your goals. By breaking through the overly linear structure of the left brain, we can get past the "shoulds." These are the goals we think we should reach: buy a Volvo, get that management position, have 1.7 kids (gifted and talented, college-track, of course) and recycle the newspapers. These are wonderful goals . . . if they're yours and not just "shoulds." Mindmapping takes you past these surface goals into the territory of your dreams. It opens up choice and freedom by breaking limiting thinking patterns.

Mindmapping is a great way to begin your goal work. Start with the perception that all things are possible. Eliminate all the barriers that say you don't have enough skill, enough time, enough money, enough energy. If you really want to do something, you will find a way around all these barriers.

Perspective and Success

Studies have shown that people who consider their lives to be happy have a common trait. It isn't the amount of money they have or even the amount of love in their lives. It comes down to their perspective. Happy people seem to notice, remember and appreciate good times more than they notice bad times. Good times are inflated; bad times tend to fade into the background. This tendency to focus on happy events and the good times also seems to generate a higher level of success.

Be the actor rather than the acted-upon

One explanation of the higher success level associated with people with this happy or positive perspective is that they feel more in control of their lives. Feeling more in control, a person becomes an actor rather than an acted-upon. The actor moves toward the goal, expecting to accomplish it. When setbacks, rejections and failures occur, they are examined for their information value and then allowed to fade. Meanwhile, the goal remains in clear view.

The perception of having it all generally includes a life in balance—family life balanced with career, material success balanced with spiritual growth, appreciation of self balanced with concern for the other people of the world and the health of the planet.

To develop more of that balanced perspective, goal work should be balanced—you should allow branches for career, family, material goods, mental growth, physical development and spiritual advancement.

Goal-Mapping Process

Find a goal-mapping partner

When you are beginning your goal-mapping process, find someone who wants to go through the process with you. This should be someone you feel comfortable sharing your goals with . . . someone who will be completely supportive when you list a goal of "buying Cuba" (an actual goal from a recent workshop) or "learning Spanish in one month." Sharing your goals not only makes them more real, but also as you hear other people's goals, you begin to realize that yours may not be so far-out after all. Goals can be for things you want to have, things you want to do or accomplish, or things you want to be.

Many groups of people are starting to form "master mind" groups. Based on the concepts of Napoleon Hill, these groups are two or more people who agree to meet at least weekly to support each other and their goals. Each member of the group sets goals and develops an action plan to meet those goals. Each week the group reviews the progress each member has made toward his goals.

Craig Case of the Franklin Institute states that only 5 percent of the people have written goals but that those with written goals are the ones most likely to succeed at their goals.

Keep a goals notebook

Keeping a notebook is an important part of your goal work. It allows you to keep your goals constantly before you, to review them, make changes and monitor how many of them you are achieving. My favorite notebook is designed by Mark Giordano and is called NoteSketch. The top half of the page is blank (perfect for mindmapping) and the bottom half is lined for more left brain activities. There is also a notebook/calendar especially designed for use with a master mind group, called the Master Mind Journal. And many of the day organizer systems have project management and goal pages. The project management section of the Franklin Institute's planning system is especially good, with materials to support mindmapping. See the Resources section for information on where to find these materials.

The Process:

"My Goals" in center of page

- Put "My Goals" or an image that represents your goals in the center of your page. (This image can be as simple as a $ or a smiley face, but it should graphically represent something you would like to move toward. Don't worry about your artistic abilities; your brain will understand it even if no one else does.) Draw branches for each important section of your life: career, family, material goods, mental growth, physical development, spiritual advancement, etc. The first goal map you do should list everything you want at any time in your life. Put down everything that has ever appealed to you . . . from learning a new language to acting in a play . . . from having a new house with a swimming pool to spending Christmas in Hawaii. Later in the process you can weed out less important goals.

Color goals:
short-term
mid-range
long-term

- Use three different colored highlighters (Pilot Pens has some wonderful colors) to highlight short-term, mid-range and long-term goals.

New maps for:
short-term
mid-range
long-term

- Make three new maps—one for each of the short-term, mid-range and long-term groups of goals. Allow all the new goals that come up in this process to be added to the appropriate map. Keep everything on your maps, even if it seems ridiculous. The only exception to this rule is if you have put something down that is negative or destructive. Once you realize that there is a better way to have your dream job than shooting your boss, it is OK to take "shooting the boss" off your map.

Highlight five top goals

- Use your yellow highlighter to highlight five goals on each map which are most important to you.
- Look at the highlighted goals on each map to see if there are any conflicts. If your long-term goal is to be a professor at Harvard and your short-term goal is to drop out of school and travel around the world, there will be a reconciliation process required! One way to get in touch with which goal is really important to you is to take a few minutes and mindmap both. Let your inner feelings come out, and you will probably find that one goal is more of a "should" which comes more from society or family than from your true self.

Action plans

- After possible conflicts have been resolved, rank each map's highlighted goals. Take the number one goal on each list and construct an action plan to accomplish that goal. Do the same for goals numbers two, three, four and five.

Goals need to be reviewed and evaluated frequently. You may want to have goals for the current year, goals for the current month, goals for the week and goals for the day. The more you have your goals identified, and written down, the more you will be focused on the action you need to take to accomplish them.

There are two pieces to success:

Two steps to success

Believing that a goal *can* be accomplished;
Believing that *you* can accomplish it.

Before Roger Bannister, it was a common belief that breaking the four-minute mile was humanly impossible. After Bannister broke that barrier, sub-four-minute miles quickly became commonplace. Runners everywhere suddenly understood that it could be done.

If you can conceive of an action plan to achieve a goal, you have step one accomplished. Step two is just following the action plan.

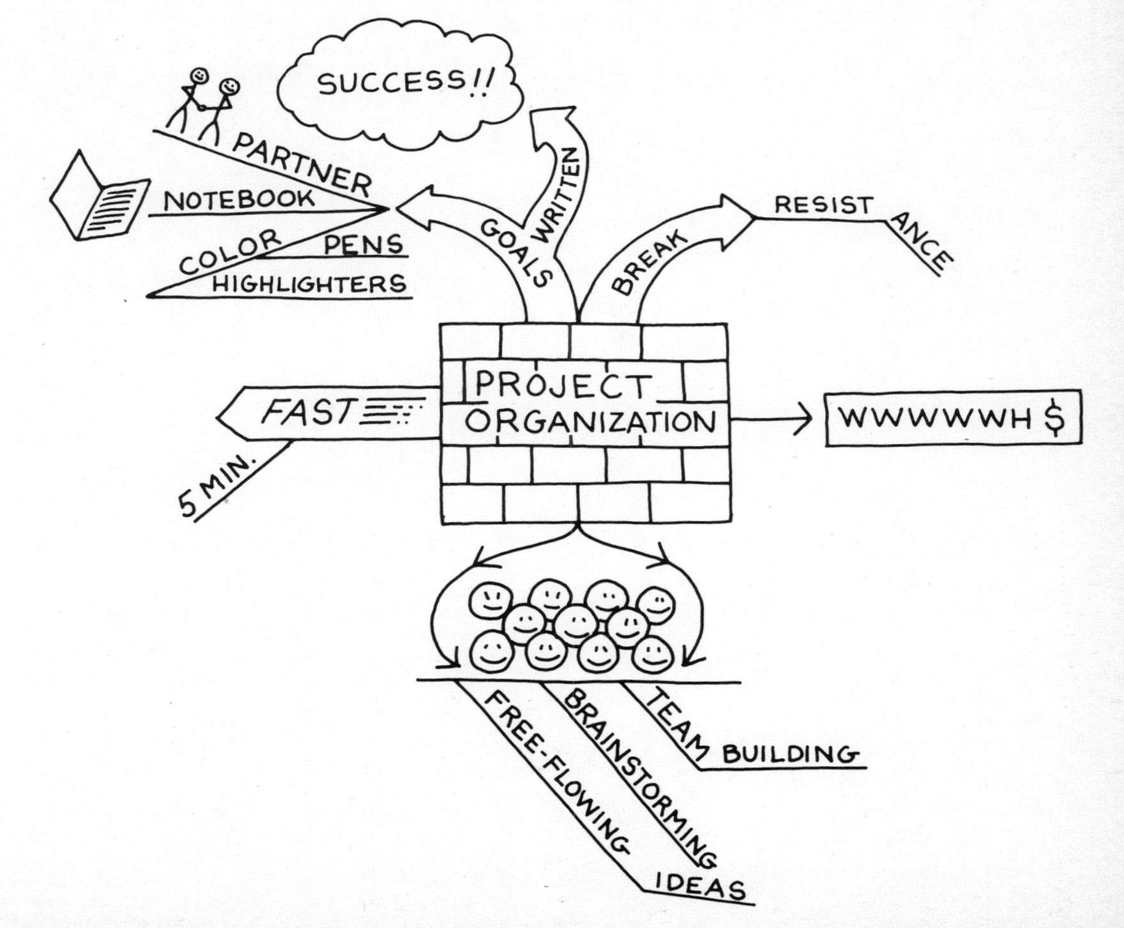

PROJECT ORGANIZATION
SUCCESS!!
PARTNER
NOTEBOOK
COLOR PENS
HIGHLIGHTERS
WRITTEN GOALS
BREAK
RESIST ANCE
WWWWWH $
FAST
5 MIN.
TEAM BUILDING
BRAINSTORMING
FREE-FLOWING IDEAS

Chapter 6: Brainstorming and Beyond

Dive into the sea of thought and
find there pearls beyond price.
—Abraham Ibn-Ezra

Brainstorming is one of the oldest creativity techniques. Developer Alex Osborn, cofounder of the advertising firm of Batton, Barton, Durstine and Osborn was conducting brainstorming sessions for BBD&O as early as 1939.

Osborn was a revolutionary thinker. Early in his career he discovered the power of ideas. Imagination became his hobby. He believed that every person possessed creative abilities and could learn to be more creative. He also felt that creative thinking was a critical part of business. He foreshadowed much of the right brain, left brain studies as he talked about the two minds: the judicial mind and the creative mind.

Osborn developed brainstorming as a way to get a group of minds focused on a single, specific problem in such a way as to generate a large number of ideas which could later be evaluated and judged. In his 1948 classic, *Your Creative Power*, Osborn listed the following rules for his brainstorming techniques:

Brainstorming "rules"

- Judgment is ruled out.
- "Wildness" is welcomed.
- Quantity is wanted.
- Combination and improvement are sought.

These same rules still guide brainstorming sessions today. Every day, businesses and organizations conduct thousands of brainstorming sessions. It would be impossible to calculate the benefit this technique has made in the quality of our lives through new products and services.

How effective is brainstorming?

In the past few years many studies have been done to evaluate the effectiveness of brainstorming. These studies found three conditions that determined the results of brainstorming sessions:

Commitment

- **Group Commitment**—Groups that are interested in the outcome of the brainstorming session are more productive than groups who have little investment in the results.

Mixed group

- **Group Makeup**—Diverse groups representing different backgrounds, skills and organizational levels were more productive than homogenous groups.

Eliminate uniformity pressures

- **Uniformity Pressures**—All groups exert a pressure toward uniformity on its members. For a brainstorming session to be effective, these pressures must be minimized. These pressures can be reduced by allowing time for individual idea generation, breaking the group into small sub-groups, realigning groups frequently, and using humor to break down communication and organizational barriers.

Enhanced Brainstorming

Here are some ways to make your brainstorming sessions more successful and more productive:

Enhanced brainstorming techniques

- **Set the Stage**—An atmosphere of accepting, freewheeling thinking is the goal. Reassure everyone that this is just the generation stage and that ideas will be later reviewed and assessed for reasonableness. Be a little offbeat and humorous.
- **Mindmap** the ideas as they flow. This helps, as it puts ideas up in a nonlinear fashion and encourages other ideas to radiate from the central focus.
- **Warm up** the group by mindmapping all the desirable outcomes that could happen if the problem being brainstormed were successfully resolved. For instance if you are brainstorming a new product, what could all of its possible benefits be? This will lead to more flexibility in thinking. It also builds the interest in solving the problem and participating in the brainstorming session.
- **Problem Definition**—The group should define the problem before proceeding with the brainstorming.
- **Start with Individuals**—Have each person mindmap possible solutions on paper. This gets the mental juices flowing and puts the group in a participation mode.

- **Have Two or Three Smaller Groups**—Use the smaller groups to generate ideas, then move back to the large group and share the ideas. Let those ideas trigger more ideas. Move back and forth between the large group and the smaller groups. This movement will add energy and humor.

- **Quotas**—After the central group maps all of their ideas, break up into smaller groups and have them generate a quota of additional ideas. This forces them into new territory. The ideas from the small groups can then be assembled and used to trigger more ideas in the large group.

- **Humor**—After the quotas have been met and everyone seems "dry" of ideas, a last round of "Stupid and Ridiculous" will usually produce a lot of laughter and some amazingly good ideas. In this round of brainstorming, you encourage everyone to think of the most "Stupid and Ridiculous" ideas possible. This should be done in the smaller groups and generally gets somewhat raunchy and energetic. After assembling these ideas, the larger group can often see ways to transform them from "Stupid and Ridiculous" to plausible.

- **Brainwriting**—A simple technique using sheets of paper divided into 21 squares (3 across, 7 down). There should be one more sheet than the number of members in the group. Each person writes an idea in each of three boxes across the sheet, then puts that sheet in the middle and takes another sheet, again writes three ideas down on it and continues until the time is up or the group runs out of ideas or energy. This method allows the ideas to bounce off of each other without specific knowledge of whose ideas are whose.

Maintain group energy

The effectiveness of a brainstorming session depends greatly on the energy level of the group. If the energy level drops, you can try a side step to revive enthusiasm and pick up the pace of idea generation. A side step is an exploration of a related aspect of the situation. If you were trying to think of a new toy for preschoolers, you might do a side step and mindmap all the classic toys of history. Or you might mindmap preschool favorites—television programs, books, food, etc.

Any side step that brings out more information related to the problem can start the mental processes churning again. If you were trying to find a new market for word processing services, you might sidestep to mindmap all users of typewriters or all the attributes of your current biggest user.

As you sidestep and gather more information, this information should be pinned up on the wall as a constant reference. Then immediately move back into the brainstorming session on your main problem.

Mindmapping and Brainstorming

Mindmapping and brainstorming work together to further encourage creativity and idea generation. Brainstorming is generally a group activity. If the results of the group idea generation are mindmapped, more ideas will be triggered as the group is able to see the ideas form organized clusters. Most brainstorming sessions list ideas in a random list form. This does not provide the organization that prompts connections and refinements.

Individual Brainstorming

Mindmapping is an excellent way to do individual brainstorming. The same rules of brainstorming apply:

- No judgment—put down all ideas.
- Quantity is wanted—analysis comes later.
- Ideas should trigger other ideas.

Any time you have a challenge, give yourself 10 or 15 minutes to mindmap possible solutions. Place the focus of the situation in the center of a page and let all your thoughts and ideas flow onto the paper. You will soon notice ideas and possibilities which have not occurred to you previously.

Exercises:

Try brainstorming any of the following situations which interest you:

How to find the money to send a child to college
How to have more fun in life
How to get a promotion at work
How to trace the family tree
What your dream house would be like
What your dream job would be like
How to develop the ideal relationship
How to lose weight or stop smoking
What to do with the backyard
What to do with all the leaves that need to be raked in the yard
What to do with all the "stuff" in the garage (attic or basement)

How to get the kids to keep their rooms neat
What to do instead of watch TV
What to do in the car while on vacation
How to learn a new skill, language, musical instrument

Try some of these . . . and have fun. See what you can come up with in just a few minutes of brainstorming.

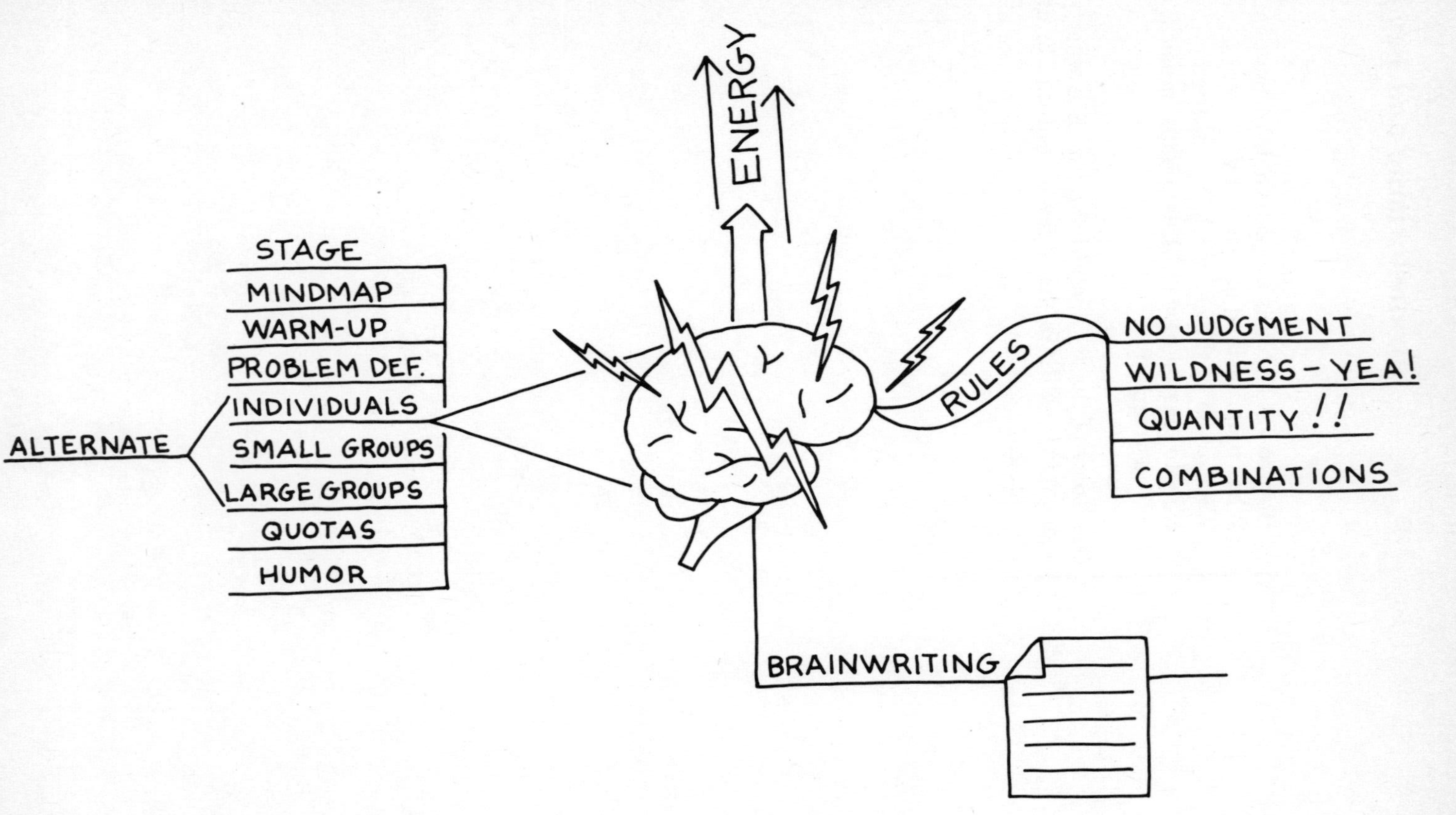
ENERGY
STAGE
MINDMAP
WARM-UP
PROBLEM DEF.
INDIVIDUALS
SMALL GROUPS
LARGE GROUPS
QUOTAS
HUMOR
ALTERNATE
RULES
NO JUDGMENT
WILDNESS - YEA!
QUANTITY !!
COMBINATIONS
BRAINWRITING

Chapter 7: Managing Meetings

If it doesn't absorb you,
if it isn't any fun,
don't do it.
—D. H. Lawrence

Projects usually involve more than one person and that leads to "MEETINGS!" Most of us recognize that meetings are necessary; however, since we have all suffered through so many boring, unproductive sessions, we shudder at the thought of another one. But meetings do not have to be boring and unproductive. They can be stimulating, challenging ways to share ideas and talents, communicate new projects and make decisions.

At a management conference many years ago, my opinion of meetings changed forever. Dr. Mason Haire was leading a seminar, and he introduced us to an exercise called "Desert Survival." In this exercise we were told that our plane had just crashed in the desert and we had salvaged 10 items. We had to decide whether we were going to walk out of the desert or stay with the airplane, and we had to rank the 10 items in order of importance. We first made those decisions individually, and then we broke up into small groups where we had to come to a consensus on the decisions.

Meetings can lead to more productivity and greater innovation

While the process of reaching a consensus was interesting, the fascinating part of the exercise was the result. When we came back to the large group and shared the results, we found that no one individual did as well as his small group. By joining forces everyone's chances of survival were improved. Prior to this exercise, I had been anti-meeting and anti-committee. The "Desert Survival" exercise taught me that the problem was the implementation, organization and direction of meetings, not the meeting process.

Recognizing Hidden Agendas

Everyone has an agenda

One way to make meetings more productive is to recognize that everyone comes to a meeting with ideas, preconceived notions and hidden agendas. Getting these out in the open early in the meeting allows more real work to be accomplished. If hidden agendas are not brought out early in a meeting, they act as a barrier to progress. Each person is only partially engaged in the meeting process because he is waiting for the opportunity to discuss his own ideas and viewpoints.

Use mindmapping to expose the hidden agendas

Peggy Smith of the San Diego County Mental Health Association always uses mindmapping to start a working meeting. She feels that this not only "warms up" the attendees, but it also gets everyone's ideas down on paper, allows and encourages everyone to participate and starts the information organization process. Getting everyone to participate is an excellent goal for a meeting planner. The primary purpose for inviting people to a meeting is to get their ideas and input. If they don't participate, you can't be sure whether they agreed with everything being said (unlikely) or whether they disagreed but were unwilling to voice their disagreement (more likely).

Mapping Meeting Goals

An excellent way to get a meeting started is to mindmap the goals of the meeting or the project on which you are working. Once you put the name of your project and the word "Goals" in the center of an easel board page or white board, you can start writing in the goals as they are given to you. It is important to write down each idea or goal that is suggested and not to allow judgment to occur during the generation process. A gentle "Let's just get all the ideas down now and we can discuss their merit later" will usually get people out of the judgment track.

Pick one goal as the meeting focus

Since the goals and ideas radiate out and around the central focus like a spiderweb, there is no hierarchy or implied ranking. After the ideas are mapped, you can ask everyone to review the map and start picking the key goals. At this point, people will pick out four or five or six goals which incorporate the high points of the project. Those goals can be highlighted with a different color so everyone can see the choices. One of our standard workshop techniques at this point is to force a selection of one goal—not as the only important goal but as the one we would like to work on for the present time.

When the group is finished with the goals, that sheet of paper can be torn off and taped to the wall so everyone can refer to it. The next step is to start thinking of ideas to accomplish the primary goal. Refer to Chapter 6 for more ideas on how to generate ideas with brainstorming techniques.

Meeting Management

Meetings are a fact of corporate and organizational life. They are the mechanism that brings people together to share information, make decisions and generate ideas. Since managers spend approximately 25 percent of their time in meetings, learning to make that time more productive can have impressive results. Careful organization and planning are essential to conducting a productive meeting. The elements of the meeting which you need to consider are:

Careful planning will make your meetings more productive and make people more willing to participate in them

People—Invite only those people who can or will contribute. Try not to get caught up in hierarchy issues such as if Joan is there, then Joe has to be. But do think through the issue and invite people who will be affected by any possible decisions.

Time—Schedule your meetings for appropriate times. Right after lunch and late Friday afternoons are not the time to get people at their best. Also, have a set beginning and ending time—and stick to them. Having a closing time for the meeting forces people to stay focused and brings issues to conclusion. Mid-to late-morning meetings are good for meetings where decisions must be made, and afternoon meetings are better for information sharing meetings where the emphasis is more social.

Agenda—A written agenda focuses you and the group. It allows the meeting attendees to be prepared. Include key questions to be addressed in the agenda, so that the attendees can begin thinking about them. Agendas also provide a mechanism for formalizing decisions. The decisions can be noted on the agenda and distributed.

Location—Make sure your room matches your group and goals. You can keep people in a stuffy, windowless conference room for an hour or so but not all day. Do you need A/V equipment? Refreshments?

Managing Decisions

Decisions need commitment and documentation

You should be especially careful of decisions made in a meeting. There is a tendency toward selective listening—the person who organizes a meeting may hear one voice agreeing with a decision and assume everyone has agreed. It's only later (when the project has been implemented and failed miserably) that the other 15 people in the room will come up to you and tell you that they thought it was doomed all along.

What can go wrong?

We have to be honest with the process and with ourselves. Give the participants a real chance to air all the possible negatives for a decision. Ask them to think of all the problems that could occur. Mindmap those potential problems on the board. This is similar to the brainstorming sessions where we try to generate new ideas. However, we are trying to think of everything that can possibly go wrong.

This process will either strengthen the original decision, as we locate possible areas of weaknesses and find way to avoid them, or it will cause us to rethink the decision all together. The bigger the project and the more risk it involves, the more time we should put into this "second look."

Take the time to hear from each person

We should also spend a few minutes soliciting the views of each person in the room to make sure that each person is actually "buying into" the decision. If it turns out that someone critical to the implementation process is not really convinced, you should spend the time necessary to reach an agreement or identify objections and reservations. The project should be postponed until the objections can be resolved.

You can force people to implement a project that they do not believe in, if you have enough authority, but the results will never be as good as if they were totally committed. This does not mean that people are sabotaging the project or being difficult. But they will not be giving the project their best unless they believe in it.

Two critical beliefs for success

There are two critical beliefs for success—the first is the belief that a project can be done. For centuries, people thought it was impossible to fly to the moon. John Kennedy believed that it could be done and his vision was passed along to millions who made it happen. The second belief is that the people involved can do the project. This belief involves resources: Is there enough time, money, equipment and personnel to do the project?

Generally objections to a project will revolve around these two success beliefs: *Can* it be done? And can *we* do it? Objections based on these beliefs can be broken down, analyzed and resolved. Another possible objection is whether or not the project *should* be done. Does it fit into the overall plan of the organization? Is it legal? Ethical?

It may take a little more time to get people's commitment. However, once everyone believes that it is the right project, that it can be done and that they can do it, the chances of success are very high.

At every step in this process, mindmapping gives you an easy, participatory technique of drawing people out, getting their ideas and inputs down on paper and stimulating communication and understanding.

Power Meetings

Generate meeting documentation as the meeting progresses

In a working meeting where you want to gather information as well as dispense it, you may want to work with a computer and transcriber. Often information is being generated faster than the facilitator can write it down. A talented transcriber can take the information which is flowing through your mindmaps and input it into specialized software (such as MaxThink for IBM PCs) to create a database as the meeting is progressing. You can then produce instant handouts (assuming your meeting room is equipped with printer and copier) which can then be reviewed and edited immediately.

With a video monitor hookup, your audience can view the information being put into the database, and much of the preliminary editing can be done before the hard copy stage. This setup also allows numerical data to be converted to graphs for easier discussion. Bernard DeKoven has published a book on this subject which discusses software and hardware requirements for power meetings. See the Resource section for more information.

Exercises:

1. Think back to the last meeting you attended. Do a mindmap on the structure of that meeting. How could it have been better? Examine the time, the place, the attendees, the agenda, the flow of information and ideas, the decisions. Did everyone participate? Were the results of the meeting clear? Did people come away with clearly stated tasks to be accomplished? Were there time schedules established?

2. Think about a meeting you need to conduct (or would like to conduct). Mindmap that meeting—the time, the place and the attendees. What is the goal of the meeting? What information do you want to share? What decisions would you like to make? Let one branch of your map be the agenda. What information should people have before attending the meeting? What information will need to be handed out at the meeting?

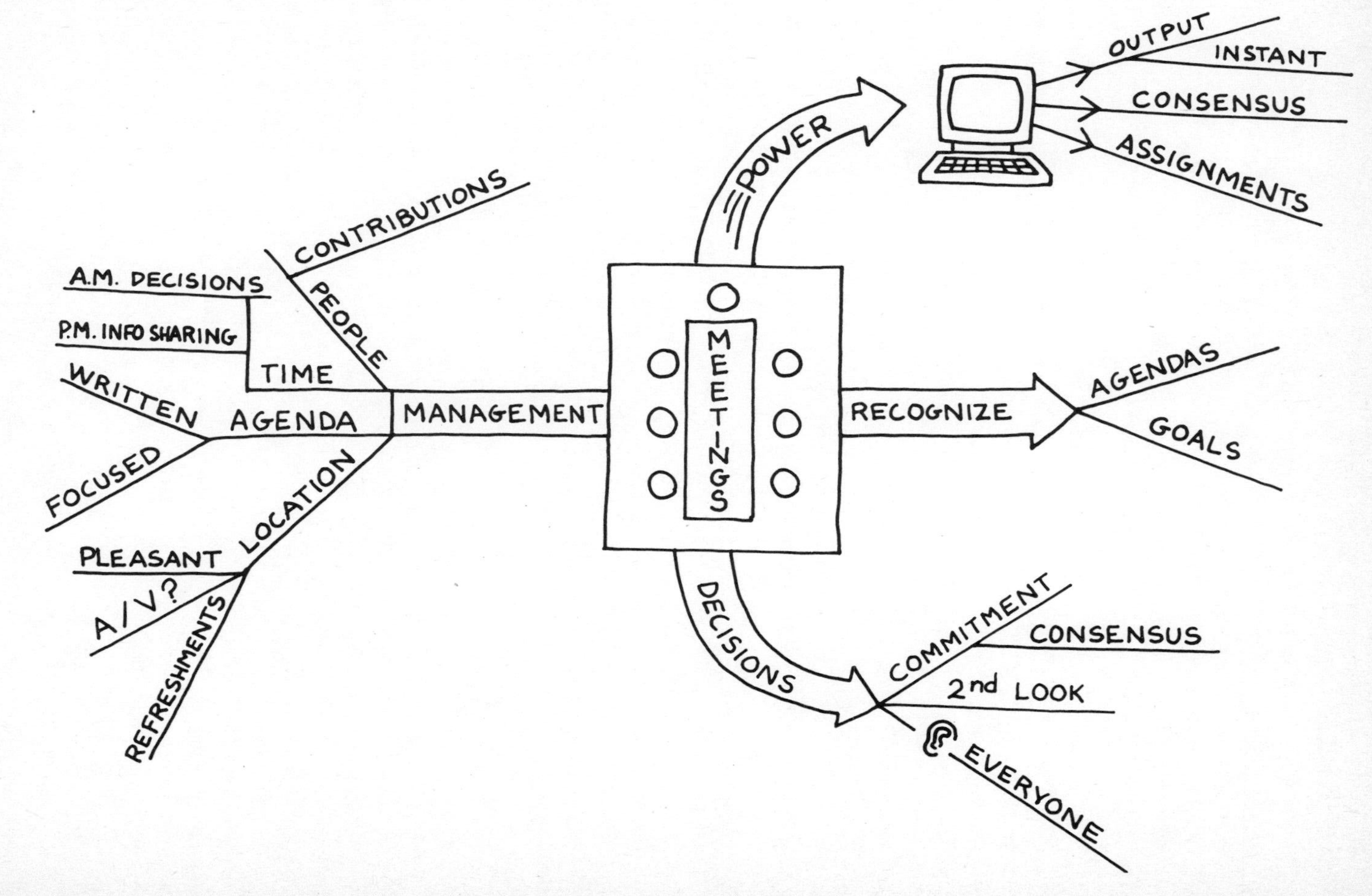
MEETINGS
MANAGEMENT
TIME
A.M. DECISIONS
P.M. INFO SHARING
PEOPLE
CONTRIBUTIONS
AGENDA
WRITTEN
FOCUSED
LOCATION
PLEASANT
A/V?
REFRESHMENTS
POWER
OUTPUT
INSTANT
CONSENSUS
ASSIGNMENTS
RECOGNIZE
AGENDAS
GOALS
DECISIONS
COMMITMENT
CONSENSUS
2nd LOOK
EVERYONE

Chapter 8: Whole Brain "To Do" Lists

If you give no thought to the future,
you can have none.
—Henry Ford, Sr.

Making a "To Do" list is one of the basic principles of time management. We know the process:

- Make a list of the tasks you want to accomplish.
- Prioritize the tasks.
- Work the list.

That's fine but in a standard day you may make it only to item 4 on a list of 15. (On a bad day, I sometimes never finish number 1!) So what do you do for the items 5 to 15? If you are on a daily system, you have to transfer everything to the next day—that's OK, but sometimes you can get one of the next tasks done in the time it takes to do all that organization. If you are on an open-ended system, you scratch off the tasks you've done, add new tasks and renumber. This is OK, but it starts to get pretty messy and it doesn't have any structure.

Why Don't "To Do" Lists Work?

Standard "To Do" lists are not flexible

Why do people buy their organizers and time management systems and still find themselves approaching their tasks haphazardly—subject to the whims of their inboxes and telephones? Why do people tell me that they sometimes fill in their "To Do" lists after the fact? And why do people stop doing these lists after the first surge of "I've got to get organized" has passed?

The simple answer is because "To Do" lists don't work the way we work. They aren't flexible . . . they don't encourage interaction . . . they aren't a part of your thinking process. They are rigid, intimidating, cold, informal and hard to maneuver. And they're black and white, linear, judgmental and not much fun!

There is a better way, and I have to thank Jesse Stewart, director of human resources at the beautiful new Sheraton Long Beach, for the idea. We were doing a team building workshop using mindmapping when Jesse suggested this as a method of doing "To Do" lists. Even though I had never used mindmapping for this purpose, it seemed to make sense, so I tried it and it is amazing! (I later learned that many mindmappers use this technique for time management, and Tony Buzan and Michael Gelb have been using the technique for 15 years!)

The only problem I've found is that I'm working harder: because I'm getting so much more done, I'm adding more and more projects to the list!

A Better Way: "To Do" Maps

Mindmapping your "To Do" list and goals puts *you* back into the process. When I used to make my "To Do" lists, I always felt that I was making them for someone else . . . almost like I would be graded or judged on my lists and how well I accomplished them. My "To Do" maps are only for me—they are messy, funny colored webs that spread all over a page. They don't mean anything to anyone except me, and they allow me to consider each part of me. They allow me to play with colors and symbols. They give me feedback and allow me to reschedule tasks without feeling like a flop.

Sunday evening is the ideal time to do your map for the week

The ideal time to map your "To Do" list is Sunday evening. By spending about 20 minutes putting your map together, when Monday morning comes you are organized and ready to go. At the end of each day, then, you only need 5 to 10 minutes to update your "To Do" map and you will be ready for the next day. Here are the basics:

- Large paper is especially good (try large computer paper or legal size paper) and several colored markers and highlighters.
- Write "To Do" and the week in a box in the center of the page. Week should be dated—July 18–24, etc.
- Think of the major groupings of your tasks (for example, a plant manager might have groupings of "Equipment," "Productivity,"

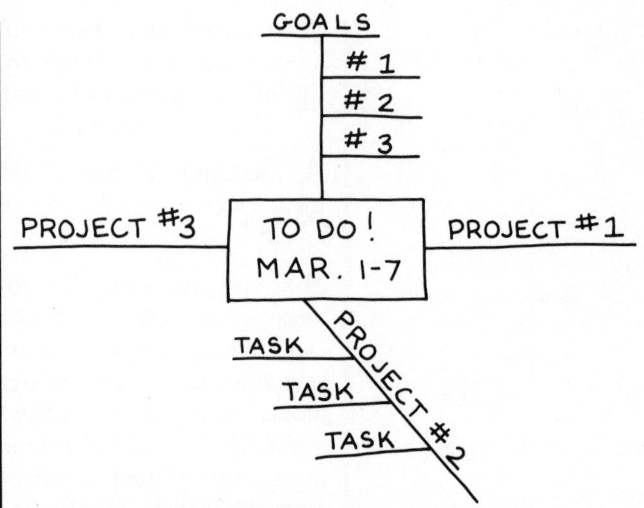

"To Do" Map with Branches

"Safety," "Administration," and "Personal," while a salesperson might have groupings of "Presentations," "Follow-up," "Proposals" and "Personal").

- The first grouping you should have, going toward the top of the page, is "Goals." You should always do this branch first as it will direct the rest of your week's activities.

- Whatever your groupings are, draw a line for each out from the box in the center, EACH IN A DIFFERENT COLOR, and write the heading of that group on the line.

- Now start writing your "to do's" on lines radiating out from the branches—in the same color as the related branch. Use key words only. Each task should take only one or two words to describe.

Highlight tasks for the day with yellow

- When you have all the tasks down that you can think of, go through them and highlight in yellow the ones you would like to finish on the next working day.
- Go through your highlighted tasks and number them in priority order. Draw a circle around the number in a different color so it stands out.
- In the upper left-hand corner, make a mark with your yellow highlighter and write the day on top of it with black ink. That shows you the correspondence between the day it is and the tasks you want to complete that day.
- As you complete a task, highlight over it in a different color highlighter–pink over yellow will create a dull orange which makes the task fade into the background.
- To get ready for the next day, you just have to highlight more tasks and renumber. You can add tasks anytime they occur to you during the day or during your review process.
- If you make a lot of phone calls, the numbers can be added next to the task. If someone isn't available when you call, marking that listing with the date and "LM" for "left message" will tell you that you called and you are waiting for a call back.
- Filing your weekly "To Do" maps gives you an excellent record of your activities.

Benefits of the "To Do" Map

You have a organized structure which gives you an instantaneous view of where you are and where you're going. It's easy to add new tasks without destroying the organization of the map. The growing spread of orange (or whatever your "finished" color is) gives you a sense of success or reward. (It's the little things in life that give us pleasure!)

You can make this map a real working tool by adding phone numbers, appointment times, etc., to your list. This is your map, and you don't have to worry about whether it gets messy or whether or not anyone else understands it.

Because this "To Do" map is more flexible, more fun and easy to use, it will be more effective than standard "To Do" lists.

Phone List Maps

Barry Farber, president of Farber Training Systems, uses phone maps. He specializes in sales training in the office automation industry, and his phone map has branches for functions such as "dealers," "regional managers," "vendors," etc. Names and phone numbers are then branched off of those functional branches. He can see his entire phone list on one page. He says, "It is much faster than having the list on a computer because I can see the whole thing at once. Also, by being able to see everyone on one page, it reminds me of people I need to call or follow up with."

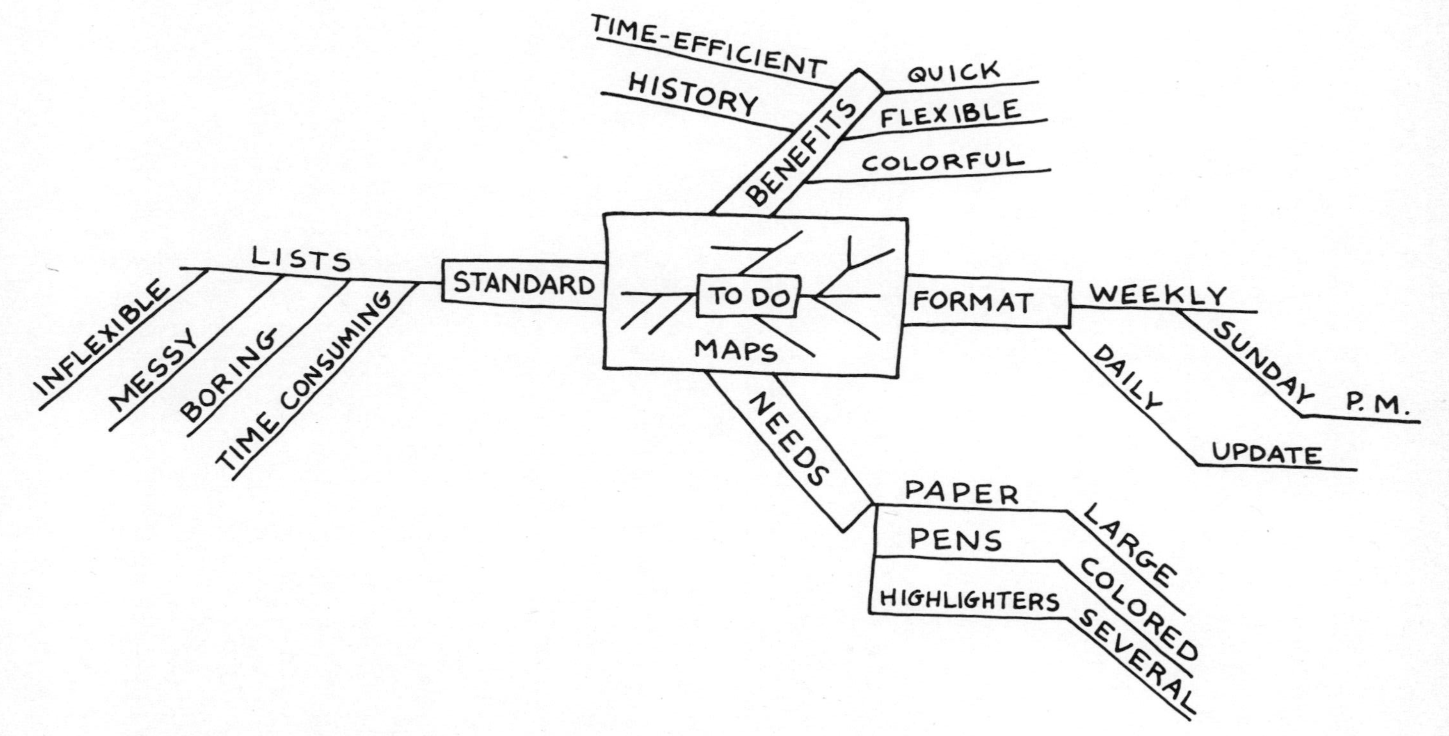

TO DO
MAPS
BENEFITS
TIME-EFFICIENT
HISTORY
QUICK
FLEXIBLE
COLORFUL
STANDARD
LISTS
INFLEXIBLE
MESSY
BORING
TIME CONSUMING
FORMAT
WEEKLY
SUNDAY
P.M.
DAILY
UPDATE
NEEDS
PAPER
LARGE
PENS
COLORED
HIGHLIGHTERS
SEVERAL

Chapter 9: Presentation Power

My father gave me this advice on speech making:
Be sincere . . . be brief . . . be seated.
—James Roosevelt

The number one fear of most adults (even more than death) is speaking in public. Yet the ability to communicate to groups of people is a skill which can make a critical difference in our careers and in our ability to accomplish our goals and dreams. The ability to share our information, our experiences and our enthusiasms with others becomes more and more important.

Speaking before a group makes us vulnerable. Failure and humiliation loom large before our eyes. When we are speaking to one person, we can hedge our bets. We can read body language and responses and change our course if we are getting into dangerous water. With a group, we are normally committed to our course, although if the tomatoes start flying we can adjust the message . . . or escape. For the most part, once a presentation starts, we are pretty much in midair and committed.

Presentations do not have to be the knee-knocking, voice-quavering ordeal that we sometimes allow them to be. Although almost every speaker, regardless of experience, still gets butterflies, most experienced speakers find that they can be made to fly in formation. There are three main principles which will allow us to control the formation of our butterflies:

- Purpose
- Improving attention and memory
- Organization

Statement of Purpose

What is your purpose?

The most important part of planning a presentation is understanding why you are giving it and why anyone would listen to it. To make sure you are not wasting your time or your audience's time, you should review why the presentation is necessary. You should be able to write a one sentence statement of purpose.

Most presentations are done to share information, educate, motivate a group to take some action or to entertain. You should know your purpose in order to prepare. Your style will be totally different if you are trying to make sure your audience thoroughly understands a new piece of legislation than if you are trying to get them to vote for the bill. The first presentation will be designed to help the audience understand and remember all the important pieces of the bill; the second will emphasize the emotional impact of the bill on the lives of the audience.

People attend presentations because they are required to or because they want something. They want information or to be entertained, or they want an experience of emotional or intellectual intensity. They do not want to be bored, conned or treated like schoolchildren.

How to Improve Attention and Memory

If we want people to remember the message of our presentation, we should know how memory works. If we want them to stay awake during the entire presentation, it is essential to understand how attention and memory work.

Memory can be greatly enhanced if a speaker uses memory supports and position wisely. Memory supports are:

Enhance memory with: supports and position

- Repetition
- Association/connection
- Intensity
- Involvement

These supports are also influenced by position. The material at the beginning and at the end of a presentation will be remembered more than the material in the middle. The limits of our memory prevent us from keeping more than seven items (plus or minus two) in our minds at one time.

Message retention formula:

Message retention formula

	Memory supports
+/−	**Position**
+/−	**Limitations**
=	**Message retention**

Repetition—This is the "tell 'em what you're gonna tell 'em, tell 'em, and tell 'em what you told 'em" school. People like to know what's coming and what to expect. However, they shouldn't hear the same words three times. The overview and the wrap-up should be rephrased summaries of the presentation. The beginning should hint at the message they're going to receive; it should whet their appetite for the main message. The wrap-up should reinforce the main points of the message and call for action.

Association/Connection—Information which can be connected to the listener's current store of information through stories or analogies will be better understood and easier to retrieve.

Intensity—Emotional content of your message is very important even if you are doing a technical presentation. Bringing in an emotional quality turns on the right brain traits and takes the message to a different level. Intensity can be added by voice quality. If you are passionate about your message, it can be reflected in your voice, by stories of people or events connected to the message and by relating the message to the lives and values of the individuals in the audience.

Presentations should appeal to as many senses as possible

Involvement—Sensory involvement is important because people have different methods of processing information. Some people are highly visual: they receive and process most information visually. Others are primarily auditory, receiving most of their information through the actual words or sounds used. Some are kinesthetic, receiving information through their feelings and emotions. Your message should be presented in such a way that it appeals to all of the senses and to each of the primary processing modes. All too often, we feel that we can get up and speak for 30 minutes or an hour and have everyone remember what we say. If we don't use each of the processing modes, some people won't even "get" the message, let alone remember it.

If you think back to the jelly dish analogy in Chapter 1, these memory supports are like making the warm water a little hotter. The hotter the water, the deeper the groove it makes when it is poured on the jelly.

Encouraging the participants to take notes or presenting the material so that it appeals to each of the senses causes the mind to absorb and retain more of the material.

First and last material is remembered most

Position—The first and last material received is remembered better than material in the middle of a presentation. There are two ways to use this fact: 1) emphasize the material you want your audience to remember in the first and last seven minutes of your talk; 2) use change-of-pace exercises to artificially create subcycles so that there are more "first and last" parts to your presentation.

Remember that the average attention span lasts no more than seven minutes and that attention starts to break down completely after an hour and a half. If you are presenting material that does not involve audience participation, you should take a 10 minute break every hour; if you have audience participation, you can take it every hour and a half.

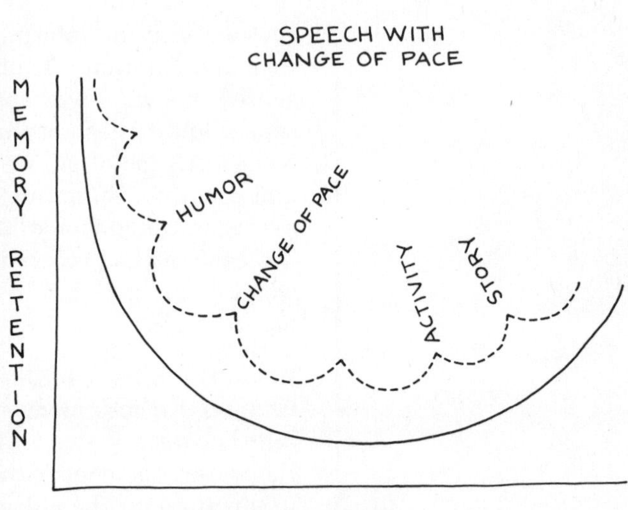

Attention Cycle with Minicycles

Recently, in a presentation for a group of physicians, I needed to emphasize the chaotic state of the medical industry. Realizing, however, that physicians had heard this gloomy material repeatedly, I put together a cartoon slide show titled "Gloom and Doom—or What Are They Going to Do to Me Next?" This presentation recapped the last two hundred years of medical practice in six minutes, got several laughs and, most importantly, brought home my message.

Change the pace every 10–15 minutes

Change Pace—By using a pace changer every 10 to 15 minutes, you can break up your talk into minitalks and keep attention riveted. Good pace changers are: appropriate humor, stories, exercises requiring people to move their bodies (even if it's just raising their hands) and calls for a verbal response. These exercises create an attention peak and start the memory cycle over again. They keep pulling the mind of the listener back to your message.

If your presentation is after lunch, these change-of-pace exercises should be as physical as possible since you are going against digestion and a natural down cycle. If you have ever nodded off during an afternoon presentation, think of what it would take to keep you awake and then use that as part of your presentation.

Organizing Your Presentation

Mindmapping can help you organize and present your material so that you take advantage of the above points. You can mindmap the material to begin your preparation. Using mindmapping at this stage will help you tap into the emotional issues involved with your material. You may even want to make "Feelings" or "Emotions" a branch so that you make sure you explore the emotional content of your subject.

Colors and symbols add interest and increase memory

When you have a presentation map that represents the presentation you want to make, you should draw it a couple of times, adding colors and symbols until you have it firmly in memory. Once you are able to draw this map, you have your notes memorized. Then you will not have to fiddle with index cards or sheets of paper. This one step will increase your confidence level enormously.

As you make your presentation, you will want to draw your presentation map for your audience. This gives them a visual structure and guides them in note taking. This map should use color and pictures as much as possible to make it visually interesting. Color can be used to represent each separate branch or you can use different colors to highlight certain ideas or to add emphasis to your main points. Some speakers make the original map in black as they're going through the "tell 'em what you're going to tell 'em" stage and then go back and use color to emphasize the current point as they're in the "tell 'em" stage.

If you are presenting information which needs to be remembered, try to keep your branches distinct and in separate segments of the page. Many people have excellent spatial memory and will remember a topic because it was the "stuff in red in the upper left-hand corner."

Mindmaps are extremely easy to use in small groups. You need only one or two easel boards and some colored markers. If you are in a larger group, you can do the same maps with an overhead projector and still maintain eye contact with your audience.

The Big Idea

What is the one idea you want your audience to "get"?

Whenever we are making a presentation, our first task is identifying ***The Big Idea***. This is the idea that we want the audience to "get" even if they don't "get" anything else. We will probably present this idea in several fashions and spend a good deal of time proving it. We may never even mention our main point specifically. However, it is critical that we know what it is and that we understand that our goal in the presentation is for the audience to "get" ***The Big Idea***.

Visual Aids Strengthen Your Message

Your second thought as you prepare for your presentation should be what visual aids to use. In addition to hearing your message, if the members of the audience can have the important points emphasized with good visual aids, their ability to remember the message will be strengthened dramatically. Human memory is very slippery; facts, details and information quickly evaporate unless reinforced.

Match your audiovisual aids to your audience

The type of audiovisual aids you use depends primarily on the material you are presenting and your audience. Here are some general guidelines:

Small, Informal Groups—White boards and easel boards allow you to present information visually in an extemporaneous manner. These aids are best for presenting relatively uncomplicated material.

Small, Formal Groups—Prepared flip charts and overhead transparencies allow complex material to be presented quickly and completely.

Large, Formal Groups—Slides are most appropriate for large meetings as they allow the widest range of graphics and provide the best quality. Careful consideration should be given to the lighting in the room. Rear projection of slides is best as it allows the room lights to be kept on.

If you need a dark room in order to get the full effect of your slides, you may want to group them into one short, visually interesting period rather than showing them throughout your presentation and trying to talk with the lights down. People go to sleep when it's dark!

Exercises:

Pretend you have been called on to make a 15-minute presentation to a club. The presentation is to be on your hobby, and you want everyone to enjoy the talk and learn about your hobby. Mindmap your hobby, letting all of your thoughts and feelings come out. Include experiences you've had or that others have had. Include your feelings while doing the hobby.

Now, using that map, make another map that you could actually use as a visual aid with the group. This map will help you remember your presentation, and it will help the audience remember what you have presented. Use different colors to highlight different areas of the presentations. Add some images (even if you don't draw well) to add interest.

Find a group and actually give this presentation.

Audiovisual Do's and Don't's

Here are some tips for the various types of audiovisual aids:

Slides:

Do:	**Don't:**
Check equipment	Turn out lights
One idea per slide	Crowd information
Dark background and light lettering	Read the slides
Six lines per slide, max	Turn your back to the audience
Six words per line, max	Distract attention with a pointer
Change slides every 15 to 20 seconds	Back up to previous slides—use copies if you need to repeat
Use build-up slides for complex points	
Use bar charts, pies	
Use special effects for emphasis	
Keep them simple	

A/V equipment only fails at the worst possible moment—check it first!

Use a title slide before each major section. Use of a standard border and logo and the same color background gives a professional, "corporate" image. When using graphs, bar charts, etc., make sure your point comes across and that the viewer doesn't have to "get" too much. Vary your slides so that you have a mixture of text, graphs, illustrations, special effects. Text should telegraph: action words, no "fluff" words. ALWAYS check equipment prior to presentation. Use remote control device if you are controlling the presentation; otherwise make sure your controller knows the script.

Overhead Transparencies:

Do:	Don't:
Make them legible	Crowd information
Use colored pens to highlight info during talk	Read from screen
Frame transparencies—use frame for notes	Turn out lights
Check alignment of screen before talk	

Limit the information you put on a transparency. What ONE idea do you want remembered?

Although you can put a little more information on a transparency than on a slide, you can't show a complete balance sheet or five year P&L and expect your audience to comprehend any part of it! Also, this is not the place to show memos or lengthy textual material. Transparencies can be excellent visual aids. If you use them a lot, you might want to check into the supplies 3M has for adding color and graphics. Well done transparencies can be as effective as slides.

Flip Charts:

Do:	Don't:
Organize in advance	Crowd information
Use color for emphasis	Read chart
Print legibly	

Flip charts are great for informal presentations because information can be penciled in and then entered later for dramatic impact—and notes can be penciled in the margins. Pages can be taped to the wall so that you can move back and forth between information segments.

White Boards:

Do:	Don't:
Use color for emphasis	Crowd information
Print legibly	
Have a designated recorder	

The trick with white boards is to have your material organized in advance. Since most white board presentations are extemporaneous, it helps if you have mentally rehearsed drawing your material. Visually organizing your material also helps your understanding. If you can draw it, you can explain it.

Handouts:

Do:	Don't:
Use them to emphasize important material	Hand them out until you want them read
Use to expand complex material	Announce in advance
Make them look professional	

People will start reading handouts as soon as they receive them

Handouts are tricky. You want to leave your audience with high quality material which will reinforce your presentation. Yet you may jeopardize your entire presentation by handing out material in advance. Your audience will read any material you hand out before your presentation begins—or, even worse, as it is beginning.

Unless you have a very large group and no assistants, it is better to hand out materials as you progress through your presentation. If your group is large, having the handouts available at the end of the presentation may be an acceptable alternative. Michael Gelb, who makes presentations an art form, recommends not telling audiences that handouts will be available, in order to keep them focused on the material as it is presented rather than relying on receiving handouts later.

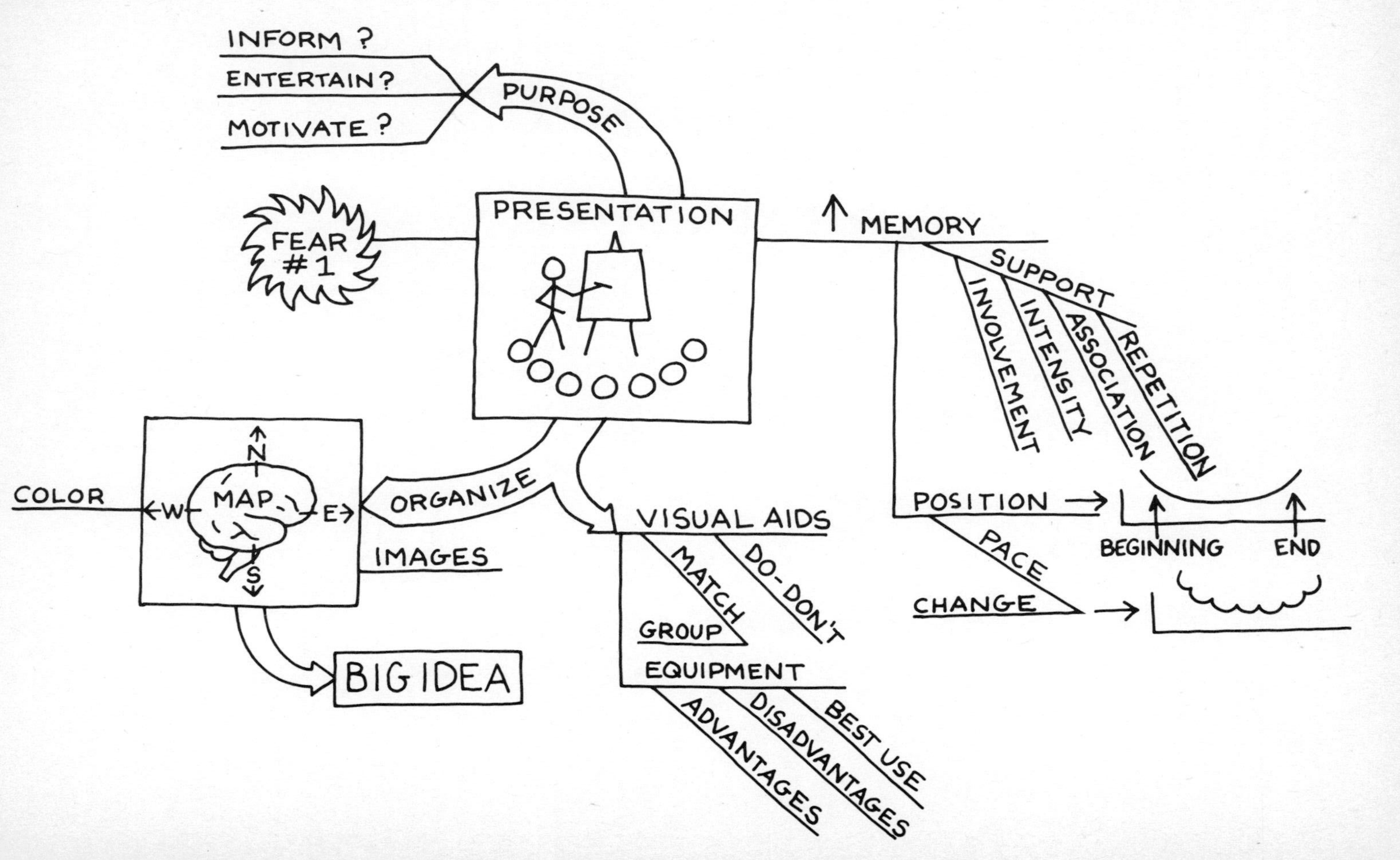
INFORM ?
ENTERTAIN ?
MOTIVATE ?
PURPOSE
FEAR #1
PRESENTATION
MEMORY
SUPPORT
INVOLVEMENT
INTENSITY
ASSOCIATION
REPETITION
POSITION
BEGINNING
END
PACE
CHANGE
COLOR
N
W
MAP
E
S
ORGANIZE
IMAGES
BIG IDEA
VISUAL AIDS
MATCH
DO-DON'T
GROUP
EQUIPMENT
ADVANTAGES
DISADVANTAGES
BEST USE

Chapter 10: Improving Learning Skills

The mind is not a vessel to be filled
but a fire to be ignited.
—Plutarch

Sixty teenagers flooded into the room—clapping, laughing and dancing. Loud, excited voices filled the air. Rock music blared in the background. The kids milled around in a chaotic energetic throng giving high fives, high threes and low fives under the knees. Whoops, yells and giggles were everywhere. The instructor called above the din for their attention. The music stopped and silence gathered as the teenagers found seats on the floor in front of him. All eyes and attention focused on the instructor, Rich Allen, a mass of energetic humor who constantly poked, prodded and encouraged the kids. Calling for a drumroll, Rich led the 60 students through a memory pegging system, one of several accelerated learning techniques taught at SuperCamp.

Music, humor and physical involvement focus attention

SuperCamp is an intense, high-energy, 10-day summer camp for teenagers which teaches learning skills in an environment rich with motivation, fun, music, support, energy and humor. On this Sunday, parents and friends of future campers had gathered for a demonstration of SuperCamp. We saw fast-paced sessions which constantly switched gears, keeping kids and parents engaged and interested. A short learning theory session would be followed by an exercise applying that theory. Each exercise offered the kids a chance to try something new. For example, the memory lesson had them reciting 12 rock bands they had just memorized, in order and then backward. Each effort was loudly supported with cheers and claps from the instructor and other campers. And, between the theory sessions there was always a physical change-of-pace exercise accompanied by energetic music. Boredom and fatigue were banished long before they had a chance to set in.

Throughout the room there were multicolored signs reading "Dream Big—Take on Life," "Everything I want is a belief away," "Learning is Fun and Easy," "If I believe I can, I can," "A failure is simply the information I need to succeed." And always there was music, whether it was soft, classical background music or rock music announcing a new session or a driving rhythm waking up the body and brain during a change-of-pace exercise. Each exercise involved sight, sound and body movements. There was total involvement. Humor, fun and surprise kept attention focused totally on the present exercise.

The Sunday afternoon demonstration of the SuperCamp concept included former campers, hopeful team leaders, parents and prospective campers—willing and unwilling. Bobbi DePorter, founder of SuperCamp, talked briefly about the purpose of SuperCamp—to teach kids learning skills which are seldom taught in the school systems, to give kids a chance to stretch their minds and bodies, and to break down mental barriers and try out new behaviors.

One day at camp is called the "I Can't Do That" day. For one complete day the kids do things their minds and bodies tell them they can't do—like climbing a 25 foot telephone poll, standing up on the very top of it and leaping into open space for a trapeze. Of course, all of the exercises are carefully coordinated for the student's safety, but the heart-thumping fear is still there. And the mind rebels, rejecting the exercise and the entire experience, until suddenly the exercise is successfully completed and an overwhelming feeling of accomplishment replaces the fear.

Increasing confidence increases learning ability

The entire 10-day experience teaches campers how to develop self-confidence, how to recognize when their barriers are only mental and how to have better personal relationships. Two-thirds of the kids have significantly higher grades after camp, and most of them report the camp experience as a major shift in their lives. At the end of the demonstration session, the floor was opened up to students to talk about what their camp experience had meant to them. The comments were heartfelt, personal and moving. They ranged from stories of increased grades to better relationships with parents and friends. One former camper said that he wasn't scheduled to graduate with his class, but when he got back from camp, he signed up for extra classes. Now he is going to graduate with his class and has been accepted at college. A teenage girl talked about her increased confidence and how it had allowed her to apply as an exchange student to Spain . . . and be accepted!

One of SuperCamp's primary learning tools is mindmapping. The students are taught to mindmap their notes as a way of quickly getting down the basics of a lecture or reading material, organizing the information and adding their own associations and thoughts. Some of the students liked mindmapping so much they taught it to other students and their teachers when they returned to their schools.

Taking notes quickly and efficiently is important, but even more important is hearing the information in the first place. Good listening skills are critical to the learning process.

Listening—The Untaught Skill

Nature has given to man one tongue,
but two ears, that we may hear from others
twice as much as we speak.
—Epictetus

If you're talking, you aren't learning.
—Lyndon B. Johnson

Listening is the first communication skill we learn as infants. It is the skill we use most as adults. And it is the one communication skill for which most of us receive absolutely no training. Our education system emphasizes reading and writing although a relatively small amount of our time is spent in those forms of communication. About a third of our time is spent speaking and even more is spent listening.

We tend to take listening for granted, assuming that hearing is the equivalent of listening. However, while hearing is a function of the ears, listening requires the involvement of the mind. Listening is an active process not just a passive reception of sounds. Listening is rarely well performed, especially in business. Horror stories abound of mistakes and errors caused by listening errors. "I didn't understand what you meant . . . I thought you said . . . You never told me . . . I didn't hear that. . . ." are all variations of listening errors.

Sperry Corporation was so concerned with listening errors that it developed a listening course and made it available to all levels of its personnel. Sperry felt that deficiencies in listening and the failures of communication it causes were a major cause of lost productivity, wasted time and inefficiencies.

Sperry's list of bad listening habits includes:

- Paying more attention to the speaker's mannerisms than to substance
- Allowing the mind to drift
- Allowing distractions to divert attention
- Overreacting to emotion-laden words
- Allowing an initial lack of interest to prevent listening

Active listening requires involvement

Mindmapping information presented in lectures, meetings or conversations requires that you get involved with the material being discussed. Active involvement keeps your mind focused, reducing the tendency for it to drift or be diverted by distractions.

Research shows that most Americans talk at about 135 words per minute, but we are capable of listening at between 400 and 800 words per minute. The difference in the rate of speaking and listening allows time for our minds to wander. But this "spare" time can be used to improve our listening skills by paraphrasing, organizing and questioning the material we are receiving.

The following keys to better listening can be used to guide your mindmapping of material:

- Pick out key points—highlight information.
- Find the speaker's focus—what is she trying to say?
- Evaluate agreement/disagreement with speaker's focus or decide what information is needed to further the decision process.
- Ask questions while listening—what is the bias of the speaker?
- Identify the speaker's conclusions—what are the ramifications?
- Find the basis of the speech—is it factual?
- Paraphrase material and add personal elaborations.
- Look for gaps—what is not being said—are certain areas being avoided?

Improving Memory with Note Taking

Taking notes can improve memory by six times

Confucius reportedly said, "*Short pencil better than long memory.*" Taking notes is a basic memory technique which can improve memory and the ability to recall information by as much as six times.

However, the standard way of taking notes usually involves writing down certain phrases or ideas in a more or less verbatim fashion. This is actually more repetition than involvement. We are repeating in a written form what we heard or saw. This form of note taking actually has many hazards:

Verbatim notes are hazardous

- Although we can listen at up to 800 words per minute, the speaker we are listening to can only speak about 135 words per minute and we can only write about 40 words per minute! Trying to take notes verbatim will cause us to miss much incoming material.
- The process of trying to remember the previous passage and write it down while listening to new material causes inaccuracies and actually interferes with thought processes.
- One of the primary purposes of note taking is to be able to review the material to increase memory. The bulk of verbatim notes is made up of nonessential words and phrases. This makes the process of review lengthy and usually prohibitive. Standard, verbatim notes give us little opportunity to add our own organization and associations. These notes make few connections with our current store of information and are, therefore, quickly "lost" or forgotten.

Mindmapping encourages associations

Mindmapping is a more efficient form of note taking. This technique of noting allows you to quickly get ideas down in key word form, to do basic organization of the material as it is given, and gives you a chance to make connections and associations. You allow yourself to get involved with the material by adding your own thoughts, ideas and feelings as you go.

Key Words—When using mindmapping to learn new material or to take notes, it is important to use key words only. Key words are generally concrete nouns or verbs. Studies have shown that the higher the percentage of key words in notes, the higher the recall.

Mindmapping automatically eliminates the bulk of non-key words and allows preliminary organization of the material received. Extracting the key words requires attention and involvement. Attention and involvement with the material increase understanding and memory. The more you are involved with the noting process, the higher your understanding and recall.

Printing the information in the mindmap has two benefits: words have a clear visual image and are easily remembered. Using one key word for your idea allows the mind to more easily make other associations. Material which needs to be quoted or remembered verbatim can be written in a column down the side of the paper.

Associations—Adding associations and connections while you are taking notes makes the material more meaningful and establishes it in your memory.

Images—Adding images and symbols in your notes activates your right brain and increases memory and retention.

In the past few years, educators have adopted mindmapping as an effective study tool. Children are learning mindmapping as early as third or fourth grade and using it to improve their learning skills, their writing skills and their organization skills.

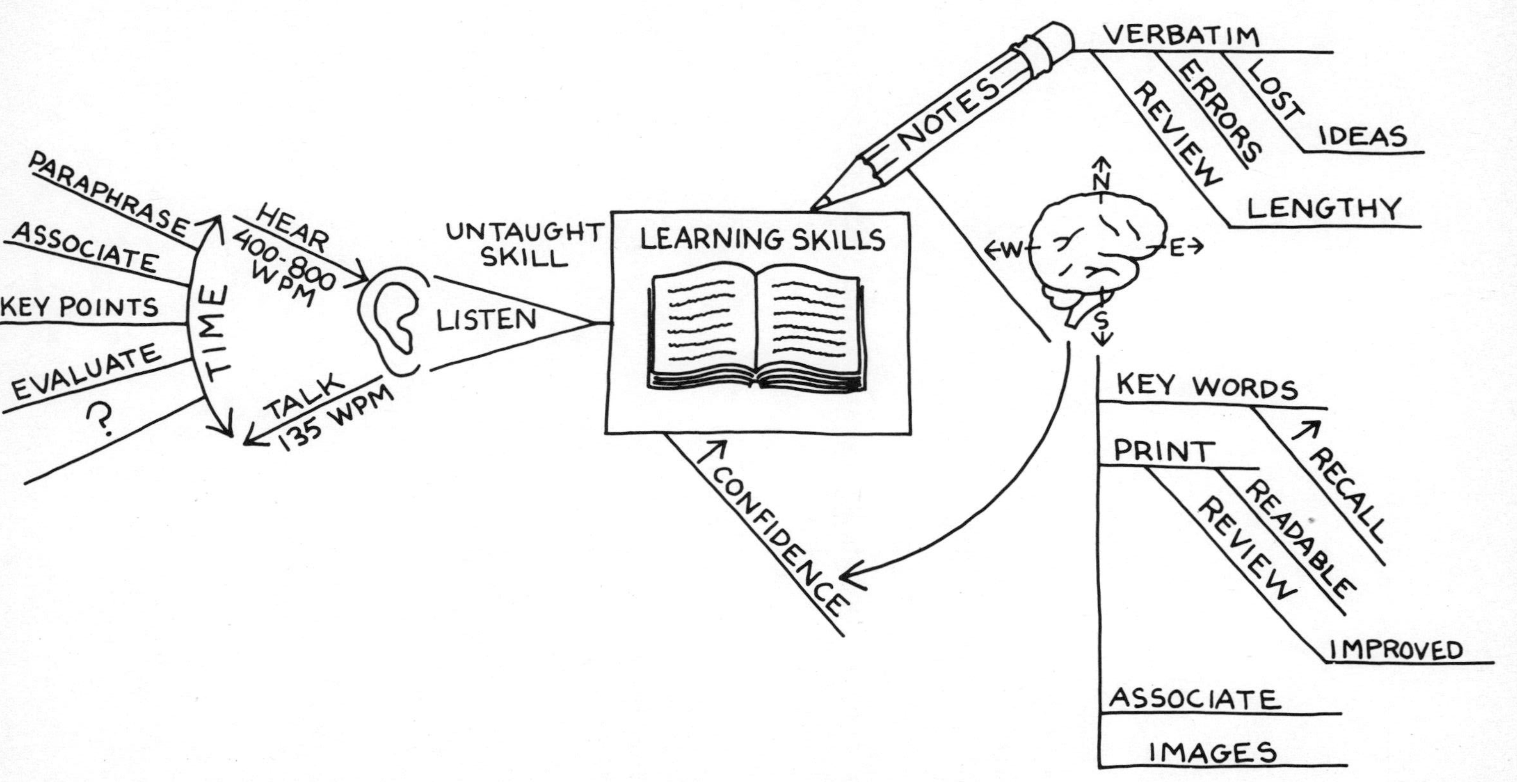
LEARNING SKILLS
UNTAUGHT SKILL
LISTEN
HEAR
400-800 WPM
TALK
135 WPM
TIME
PARAPHRASE
ASSOCIATE
KEY POINTS
EVALUATE
?
NOTES
VERBATIM
LOST
IDEAS
ERRORS
REVIEW
LENGTHY
N
E
S
W
KEY WORDS
↑ RECALL
PRINT
READABLE
REVIEW
IMPROVED
ASSOCIATE
IMAGES
↑ CONFIDENCE

Chapter 11: Mindmapping for Personal Growth

Every individual is a marvel of unknown and unrealized possibilities.
—Goethe

Because the process of mindmapping taps into deep areas of your mind and allows free association, it operates somewhat like psychotherapy. While it is not a treatment for major psychological disturbances, it can help us so-called "normal" people better understand who we are and how our minds operate. It provides us with a tool for listening to ourselves . . . for hearing the internal dialog which constantly plays through our minds. Using mindmapping in a personal journal approach can help us develop our creativity.

Our "uniqueness" leads to our creativity

It is the moving closer to an understanding of who we are and what our uniqueness is that moves us toward our creativity. Our ability to be creative depends entirely upon our ability to express and utilize our unique set of talents, perspectives and experience. By developing ourselves, we develop our creativity.

Tristine Rainer in her book, *The New Diary*, stresses writing rapidly and without censorship in order to make the journal writings meaningful. This means finding ways around our left brain censor. Mindmapping allows us to bypass that censor and touch our inner feelings and thoughts. A common way to begin the journal process is to mindmap a subject or thought as the opening portion of the journal and to let that map lead into the journal writing. Mindmapping your journal first allows you to "clear the debris" from your mind and free-associate quickly.

"Garbage" writing

Most people who begin journals have trouble opening up and getting to interesting material. They bore themselves and then think they have nothing to say. Each of us has a lifetime of thoughts, feelings and observations which can be expressed in a journal. It is only our ego which stands between us and a richer understanding of who we are. We can trick ourselves past this ego guard several ways. One method is "garbage" writing, where we just let the words flow onto paper without trying to make any sense of the words or the structure. This is a wonderful, liberating thing to do occasionally. However, most of us who are strongly left brain and judgmental will be leary of this method if it doesn't eventually lead somewhere.

Mindmapping accomplishes a similar effect . . . only faster. You're letting your mind dump and free-associate, but you're writing only the key words. When you reach that "aha" feeling you know you have a subject that you want to write about.

Mindmapping opens up our emotional "right brain"

When you mindmap a situation in your life, you are also more likely to get to the real issues underlying the situation. Because mindmapping touches the emotional right brain portion of the brain, you are more likely to evoke the feelings and emotions involved. Most of us are trained to avoid showing our feelings, so we are reluctant to pour those feelings out in our journal. This leads to a tendency to construct a chronological journal of our activities. The purpose of the personal growth journal is not to construct a history. It is to get in touch with our real feelings and thoughts. Most of us do not lead lives that are interesting enough to support the historical approach, so we get bored and quit.

Find the most important thought or feeling of the day

Anais Nin, one of the outstanding journalists of our time, realized that many of her most important childhood experiences had been omitted from her journals. She developed the habit of sitting quietly for a few minutes before beginning to write. She would allow the most important incident or feeling of the day to come to mind. She used that feeling or incident as her first sentence.

Your personal growth journal can become a fascinating account of the major changes in your life. Ira Progoff in *At a Journal Workshop* writes:

> The growth of a human being consists of so many subjective experiences, hidden and private to the person, that the markings of change are difficult to discern. Especially misleading is the fact that the active germination of a growth process often takes place at the low, seemingly negative, phase of a psychological cycle. Thus, at the very time when the most constructive developments are taking place with a person, his

outer appearance may be depressed, confused, and even disturbed.

Progoff says that the journal gives us a method of developing the necessary abilities to face the trials of life. "It gives us a means of private and personal discipline with which to develop our inner muscles."

Journal Process:

1. **Get a notebook.** Although any high quality notebook or journal will do, NoteSketch (see Resources) has developed a special notebook which is perfect for mindmapping and writing. The top half is blank and the bottom half has lines.

2. **Sit in a quiet, comfortable place** with your notebook and allow yourself a few quiet moments to focus on the most important feeling or thought you have.

3. **Write that focus in a box** (If you can think of a way to represent your focus graphically, you will get deeper into your "right brain") in the center of your page and mindmap that thought. Make sure you allow all of your thoughts to be expressed in your map.

4. **When you have an "aha**—that's what I want to write about" feeling, write down all your thoughts and observations.

Discovering Our Values

The dictionary defines a value as a principle, standard or quality considered worthwhile or desirable. Values are the beliefs and convictions which give meaning to our life. They give us direction and guidance. Yet, in the crush of day-to-day life, most of us have little time to spend thinking about our values. This was graphically brought home to me when I started trying to define my values. As I was working through a series of exercises, I realized that it was the first time I had ever thought about values in an organized manner. Later when this exercise was added to mindmapping seminars, I found most participants were also fuzzy about exactly what their guiding values were.

What are our values?

It seems incredible to me that something as important as knowing what values we live our lives by should be left undefined. We spend the early part of our lives learning values . . . from our parents; from our schools and churches; from our community and peers; from television, newspapers and music. But at some point we need to sort out what we've learned.

We need to decide which values are really critical to us and which ones may no longer have relevance. Most of us feel as if we know our values. I know if someone had asked me prior to this experience, I would have said, "Of course, I know what my values are." But after spending several hours defining, redefining, ranking and reranking, I made some major breakthroughs in understanding what I wanted from my life.

Knowing what our values are allows us a great deal of freedom. We can begin to eliminate unnecessary activities and expectations from our lives. If we examine our values and realize that what we value most in life is our family and friends, we can quit feeling like a failure if we don't get that top management position. By ranking our values, we know where to direct our energies. We can also be more honest with ourselves, more true to the self within us. A friend recently examined her values and realized that one of her most important values was expressing her creativity through music. She is a successful entrepreneur with a growing computer systems company, and her life is filled with family, friends and an interesting career, but she had been feeling empty and unfulfilled. When she realized how important music was to her, she was able to rearrange her priorities to allow music back into her life.

Life has a momentum of its own, and it carries us along on its stream unless we take some control of where we are going. If we allow ourselves to be carried along on a stream which doesn't match our values . . . our inner desires . . . we can find ourselves headed for the rocky shores of mid-life crisis, divorce, career burnout, ulcers, substance abuse and other symptoms of life out-of-balance. When our actions and activities match our innermost beliefs and desires, we reach a state of balance and peace.

Matching values and activities leads to peace and harmony

Values are our guidance systems. They drive our activities and choices, from the schools we attend to the jobs we choose, from the friends around us to the books we read, from the way we discipline our children to the way we set our tables. Values carry a strong emotional content; they are the beliefs we live for and the beliefs we die for. Common values are love, friendship, family, honesty, truth, trust, success, freedom, accomplishment, joy, abundance, wealth, travel, beauty, art, music, poetry, nature, generosity, sharing, fairness, security, adventure, and so on.

The next step to knowing our values is to find every belief, principle and condition that is important to us. As mindmapping helps us get to the inner us, it is an excellent tool for defining and ranking our values.

Mindmap all the values that are important to you

In the center of a page, draw a box and write "My Values" and let yourself mindmap all of the things that are important to you. Write quickly and put down everything. Relate ideas to each other as you notice the connection. As your energy fades, ask yourself the following questions:

- What is important to me?
- What makes me happy?
- What is there in my life that would leave a hole if it were gone?
- If I could give any quality to my life, what would it be?
- If I could give any quality to the world, what would it be?
- What qualities do I admire most in my best friend?
- What excites me?

You probably now have a pretty busy mindmap. As new ideas come to you, you can always come back and add, change or subtract. This is your value map and you can update it as often as you like. But it should now look like a listing of everything that touches your life or that you would like to touch your life. Take a few minutes and connect the values that relate to each other. You may have listed love, family and friends separately and now want to tie them together. Try to tie all your values together into several main branches.

Organize values into branches

After you have connected your values, redraw your map, using your main branches and linking all the values to those branches. Use a yellow highlighter to highlight the branches. With a different color, highlight the most important subbranch of each branch.

The hard part: ranking your values

Now for the difficult part. Look at the yellow highlighted values and rank them. This gets tricky because you may tend to come up with a lot of shoulds, "I should rank love higher than wealth. I should rank country higher than sex." (Did you even allow yourself to put sex down?) The purpose of the process is to discover what's important to you, not what what you think *should* be important. If you try to live your life according to the shoulds, you cannot be true to your real self. Being false to who we really are prevents us from growing and reaching our creative nature.

To find joy and happiness in our lives, we must come to honor the people we are. Values are changeable, and we may eventually come to highly value some of the *shoulds*, but we are dealing with our "right now" values.

So, in order to find our real ranking, look at each value in relation to the others. For example, if you had five main branches of

love ______
wealth ______
travel ______
fame ______
adventure ______

you would say to yourself, "In order to be truly happy and fulfilled, do I need love more than wealth . . . more than travel . . . more than fame . . . more than adventure?" As you get a yes or a no on each of these questions, you begin to rank the values. If you got all "yes's" on love, it would be number 1.

But if you got to fame and got a "no," you would know that fame is more important than love. You would then go through the rest of the list with "fame" and if you got "yes's", it would be number 1.

Once you have finished the ranking, spend some time thinking about how all of these values interact. Could you live without any of them? Is there anything in your life that you feel you couldn't live without that isn't up there? Are some of your values symbols for something else? For instance, do you want wealth so that you can travel? Then perhaps your wealth value is really a travel value. Do you want fame so people will love and admire you? . . . Perhaps you are really looking for achievement, or self-love, or friendship. Examine each value to see if that is what you are really looking for.

Draw a picture of your values

Spend the time it takes to work and rework this value map till it feels right. Now try to come up with a picture of your values. As I was doing this exercise, I realized that some of my values were requirements at a certain level, but they weren't ultimate values. These values of health, money, time and courage became the legs of a table. In order to have all the other values of my life, I had to have an underlying level of trust and truth. These became the top of the table. My overall value I wanted for my life was *joy*, and this became a bowl that held all the other values. You can see my value drawing on page 157. (It has been cleaned up by an artist, so don't feel that your drawing has to be artistically impeccable.) The important part of this drawing is how you see your values relating together. What is most important? What must you have so that everything else can exist? What is your overriding value?

When I was drawing my values, I made four or five drawings before an image came together that fit the relationship. So play with this exercise and let your inner self express the truth in your values.

Once your picture is completed, go back to Chapter 5 and look at your Goal Map. Does the new understanding of your values change any of your goals? Make any changes in your Goal Map which seem to be appropriate.

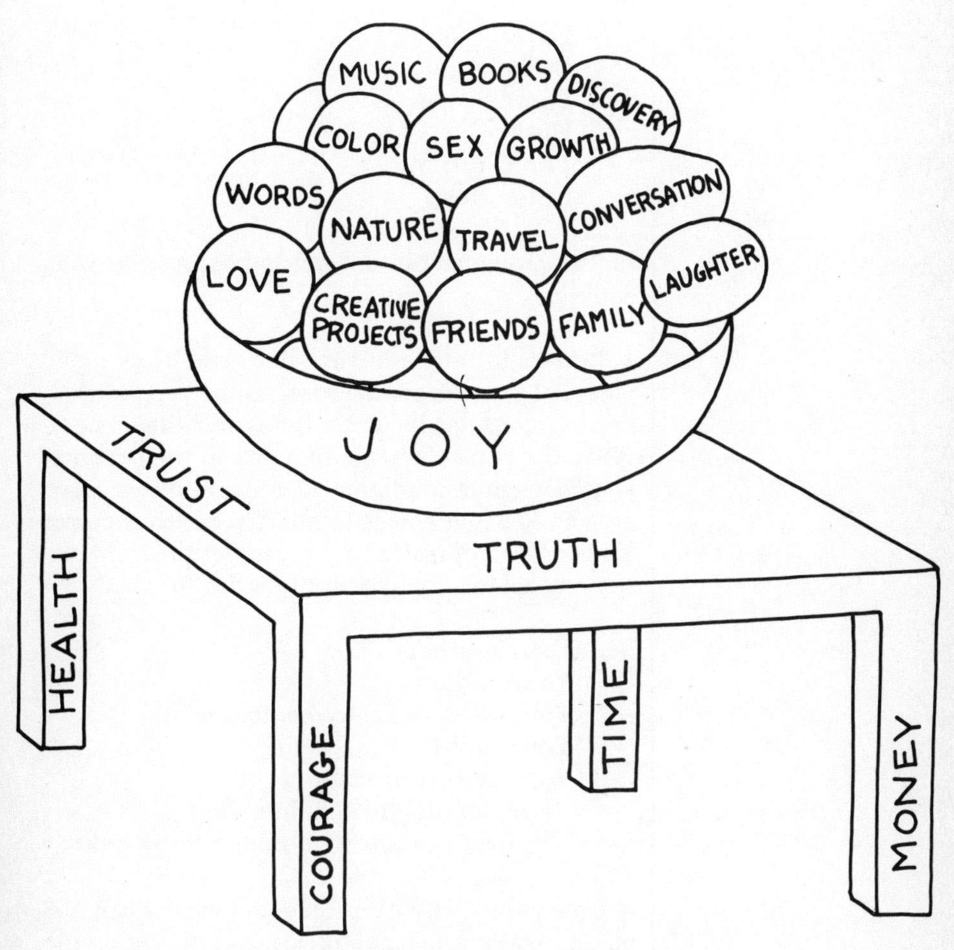

Author's Table of Values

Exercises:

1. If you are having trouble coming up with a focus to write about in your journal, try mindmapping one or more of the following:

Fear
Love
Birthday
Family
Hate
The Child Me
Inner Deep

Let each one lead into a writing expressing your feelings.

2. Letters to people in your lives can be dynamic pieces of your journal. These can be people who are living or dead, currently in your life or not. Place the person's name in a box in the center of your page and mindmap for a few minutes every association that comes to mind about that person. Then allow yourself to write the letter. Here are some people you may want to write to:

Your mother
Your father
Your ex-spouse, lover, friend
Your child
Your sister, brother
Your wonderful teacher
The first person who broke your heart

3. Conversations with people and events can also be an excellent journal device. Again, the people can be living or dead, present or distant. This exercise has the advantage of being two-sided. You

actually have the other person (or event or object) speak back to you. If you like this form of journaling, be sure to see Ira Progoff's *At a Journal Workshop.*

Dream Log

Dreams are often called the doorway to the unconscious. Recording our dreams is an important part of the process of getting in touch with our inner selves. However, recalling and recording dreams is often difficult, as they slip away like smoke between our fingers.

Ann Faraday suggests that the forgetting of our dreams is not so much because of a Freudian-type repression but more because of the state of our brain. During sleep, our brain does not lay down strong memory traces. Therefore, it is important to catch these illusive images quickly, before other images have completely overlaid them.

Mindmapping helps capture our dreams

Mindmapping provides a technique for locking in the image. In order to record your dreams, you should keep a dream log beside your bed. Before going to sleep, tell yourself that you intend to remember your dreams. The best times to capture the illusive dream images are immediately upon awakening when you are still in the twilight between completely awake and completely asleep. Before talking, getting up or anything else, you should keep your eyes shut and review the images of the dream. Then put the central image of the dream on paper and mindmap that image. Your associations can be from the dream or associations which come up from the dream images. Once you have captured the essence of the dream you can wait until later before analyzing the dream. Michael Gelb states that a recent study where students recorded their dreams showed an increase in creativity of 25 percent. He states, "Mindmapping bridges the gap between the image-rich, apparently illogical, dream world and our more verbal waking consciousness."

Analyze each dream element as a piece of yourself

Some dream workers suggest thinking of each element of the dream as a piece of yourself. Therefore, if you had a dream of a little bird sitting in the rain on a branch outside your window, you would think of "the little bird that is me" sitting on the branch and see what associations or thoughts come from that image. You can then examine the "rain that is me" image, the "branch that is me" and the "window that is me." Each piece of the dream is a reflection of some aspect of us. Only by analyzing the dream ourselves can we learn the message our subconscious is sending through the dream.

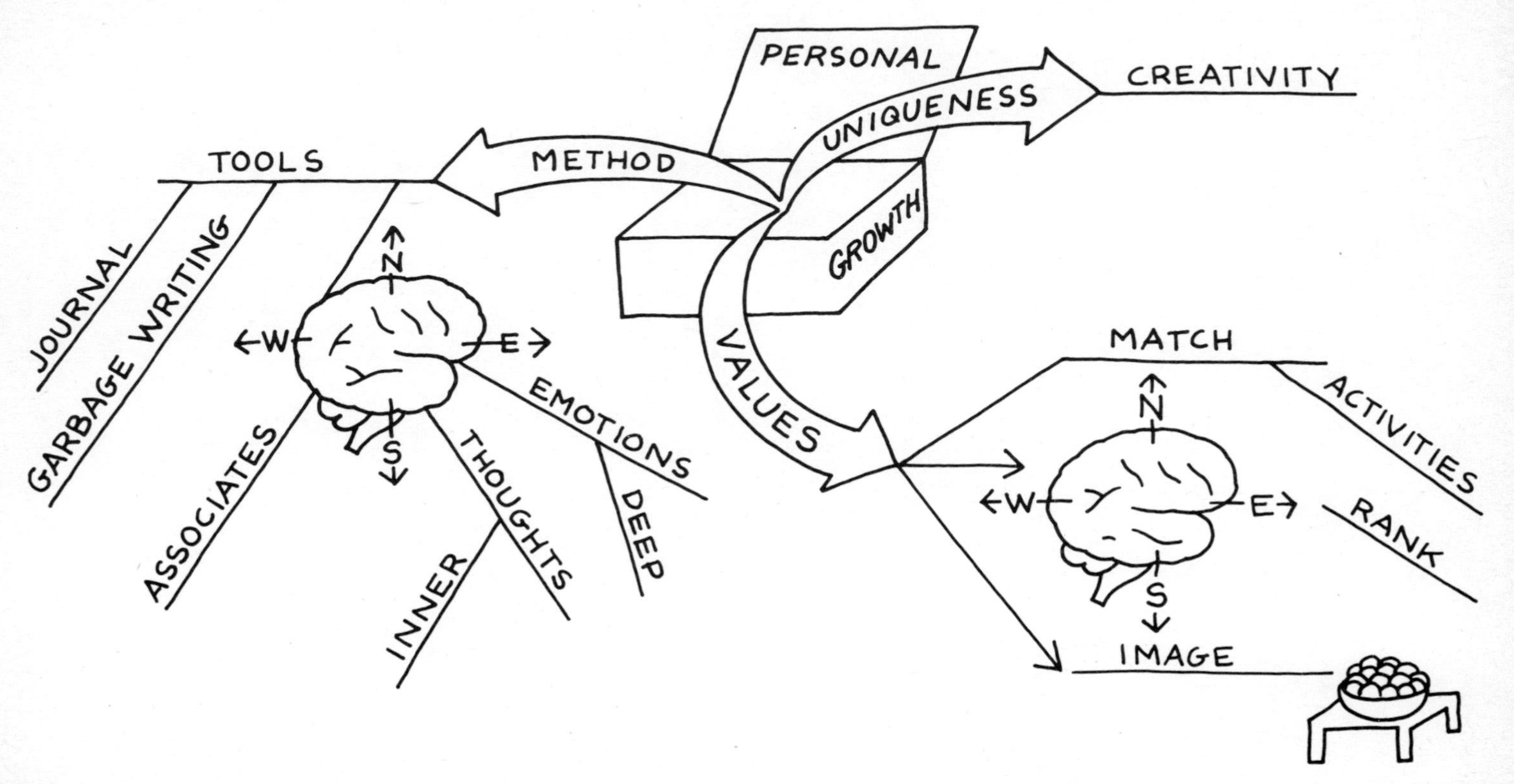
PERSONAL
GROWTH
UNIQUENESS
CREATIVITY
METHOD
TOOLS
JOURNAL
GARBAGE WRITING
ASSOCIATES
N
W
E
S
EMOTIONS
DEEP
THOUGHTS
INNER
VALUES
MATCH
ACTIVITIES
RANK
N
W
E
S
IMAGE

Conclusion

Mindmapping has helped thousands of people understand better how their minds work. It has helped them be more productive when organizing projects, speeches, presentations and meetings. It has brought more depth and color into their writing, easily sweeping away writer's blocks. And this simple tool has helped people to appreciate a little more their unique perspective and experiences.

When I first started using mindmapping 10 years ago, I was working in accounting and finance. I prided myself on my logic and practicality and had a rigid view of what was professional. (I once told a secretary in our office who used green ink that I thought it was unprofessional.) I had tried visualization but never seemed to "get" anything.

Mindmapping was presented to me as a way of getting more organized. I tried it and it worked. I could get projects organized faster and my time management improved. But other things started to change also. New ideas started popping up faster. I started to enjoy playing with color in the mindmaps. As I started to notice these changes, I wanted to know more about the mind and how it works. I became especially fascinated with innovation and creativity and began to study the leading thinkers in this area. As an exercise for a graduate class, I designed a two-day workshop on creativity. I was so excited by the workshop that I got permission to present it to my coworkers.

While the workshop was fun and stimulating, the one technique that everyone loved was mindmapping. People made breakthroughs when they learned this simple technique. I started teaching it at the local colleges and then for businesses as a way of developing new products and services, encouraging teamwork, fostering innovation and managing projects better.

Once people start to open up to the possibility that they are creative—that they have potential that they weren't aware of—they make dramatic breakthroughs. You are smarter than you think you are and more creative than you ever thought possible. Mindmapping can help you discover your hidden potential.

I encourage you to try this technique and would love to hear from you—your successes and your failures as you explore it. Please feel free to send your questions, stories or comments to me at: 1103 Harbor Hills Dr., Santa Barbara, CA 93109.

Happy Mindmapping!

Resources

Corporate Creativity Training:

Tony Buzan
Buzan Centre
Cardigan House, Suite 2
37 Waterloo Rd.
Winton Bournemouth
Dorset, UK BH91BD

Michael Gelb
High Performance Learning
4613 Davenport St., NW
Washington, D.C. 20016
1-202-537-0775

Stan Gryskiewicz
Center for Creative Leadership
Post Office Box P-1
Greensboro, NC 27402-1660
1-919-545-2805

Joyce Wycoff
MindPlay
1103 Harbor Hills Dr.
Santa Barbara, CA 93109
1-805-962-9933

Color:

Wagner Institute for Color Research
111 West Valerio Street
Santa Barbara, CA 93101

Notebooks, Journals, Organizers:

NoteSketch
820 East Sparrow Road
Virginia Beach, VA 23464
1-804-420-4004

The Franklin System
The Franklin Institute
Box 25127
Salt Lake City, UT 84125-0127
1-800-654-1776

Universal Personal Organizer
c/o Buzan Centre
Cardigan House, Suite 2
37 Waterloo Road
Winton Bournemouth
Dorset, UK BH91BD

Miscellaneous:

Bernard DeKoven,
C-EM Publications
2972 Clara Drive
Palo Alto, CA 94303

Publisher of *Power Meetings: An Introduction to Computer-Enhanced Meetings*

MaxThink (Software)
44 Rincon Road
Kensington, CA 94707

Powerful, outlining and organizing software.

The Mind Map
High Performance Learning
4613 Davenport St., NW
Washington, D.C. 20016

A colorful poster that gives you complete guidelines for mindmapping.

SuperCamp
1725 South Hill Street
Oceanside, CA 92054
1-800-527-5321 or
1-619-722-0072

A powerful, accelerated learning camp for teenagers.

Bibliography

Chapter 1: The Mind's Unknown Potential

Chamberlain, P.h.D., David B., *Consciousness at Birth: A Review of the Empirical Evidence.* Chamberlain Communications: San Diego, CA, 1983.

De Bono, Edward, *Lateral Thinking.* Harper & Row: New York, NY, 1970.

Hermann, Ned, *The Creative Brain.* Brain Books: Lake Lure, NC, 1988.

Hooper, Judith, and Teresi, Dick, *The Three-Pound Universe.* Macmillan Publishing Company: New York, 1986.

McKim, Robert H., *Thinking Visually: A Strategy Manual for Problem Solving.* Lifetime Learning Publications: Belmont, CA, 1980.

Minsky, Marvin, *The Society of Mind.* Simon and Schuster: New York, 1985.

Ornstein, Robert, and Thompson, Richard, *The Amazing Brain*. Houghton Mifflin Company: Boston, 1984.

Russell, Peter, *The Brain Book*. E. P. Dutton: New York, 1979.

Chapter 2: Creativity—Within Each of Us

Campbell, Ph.D., David, *Take the Road to Creativity and Get Off Your Dead End*. Center for Creative Leadership: Greensboro, NC, 1985.

Feldman, Beverly Neuer, *Kids Who Succeed*. Macmillan Publishing Company: New York, 1987.

McKowen, Clark, *Thinking About Thinking*. William Kaufmann, Inc.: Los Altos, CA, 1986.

Ray, Michael, and Myers, Rochelle, *Creativity in Business*. Doubleday & Company, Inc.: Garden City, NY, 1986.

Von Oech, Roger, *A Whack on the Side of the Head*. Warner Books: New York, 1983.

Chapter 3: Mindmapping—Whole Brain Thinking Technique

Mindmapping:

Buzan, Tony, *Use Both Sides of Your Brain*. E. P. Dutton, Inc.: New York, 1974.

Gelb, Michael J., *Present Yourself!* Jalmar Press: Rolling Hills Estates, CA, 1988.

Russell, Peter, *The Brain Book*. E. P. Dutton: New York, 1979.

Mind Exercises:

Ostrander, Sheila, and Schroeder, Lynn, *Superlearning*. Laurel Books: New York, 1979.

Raudsepp, Eugene, with Hough, George P., Jr., *Creative Growth Games*. Harvest/HBJ: New York, 1977.

Raudsepp, Eugene, *More Creative Growth Games*. Perigee Books: New York, 1980.

Raudsepp, Eugene, *Growth Games for the Creative Manager*. Perigee Books: New York, 1987.

Wujec, Tom, *Pumping Ions, Games and Exercises to Flex Your Mind*. Doubleday & Company: Garden City, NY, 1988.

Chapter 4: Writing Can Be Easy, Effortless and Enjoyable

DiGaetani, John L.; DiGaetani, Jane B.; and Harbert, Earl N., *Writing Out Loud, A Self-Help Guide to Clear Business Writing*. Dow Jones-Irwin: New York, 1983.

Holcombe, Marrya W. and Stein, Judith K., *Writing for Decision Makers*. Lifetime Learning Publications: Belmont, CA, 1981.

Howard, Ph.D., V. A., and Barton, J. H., *Thinking on Paper*. William Morrow & Company: New York, 1986.

Waterman, Jr., Robert H., *The Renewal Factor*. Bantam Books: New York, 1987.

Chapter 5: Better Project Management

Bennett, Robert F., *Gaining Control, Your Key to Freedom and Success*. The Franklin Institute, Inc.: Salt Lake City, UT, 1987.

Chapter 6: Brainstorming and Beyond

Adams, James L., *Conceptual Blockbusting, A Guide to Better Ideas, 2nd edition*. W. W. Norton & Company: New York, 1980.

Osborn, Alex, *Your Creative Power, How to Use Imagination to Brighten Life, to Get Ahead*. Charles Scribner's Sons: New York, 1948.

Chapter 9: Presentation Power

Gelb, Michael J., *Present Yourself!* Jalmar Press: Rolling Hills Estates, CA, 1988.

Chapter 10: Improving Learning Skills

Montgomery, Robert L., *Listening Made Easy*. AMACOM: New York, 1981.

Chapter 11: Mindmapping for Personal Growth

Faraday, Ann, *Dream Power*. Coward, McCann & Geoghegan, Inc.: New York, 1972.

Progoff, Ira, *At A Journal Workshop, The Basic Text And Guide For Using The Intensive Journal*. Dialogue House Library: New York, 1975.

Rainer, Tristine, *The New Diary, How To Use A Journal For Self Guidance And Expanded Creativity*. Jeremy P. Tarcher, Inc.: Los Angeles, CA 1978.